This anthology is a cu. ~~...~~ *~~is just~~*

disappearing from the memory of most Jamaicans. What is often overlooked from those times was the quality of life which simple rural folks enjoyed; as many from that era can recall, "life was so simple and yet so fulfilled."

Linley guides his audience to see and feel the imageries he is conveying to them. I wholeheartedly endorse this iconic literary and cultural masterpiece, which will no doubt be reckoned with similar works in the National Library!

Rev. Dr. Orville K. Neil
Author and Former Minister,
Moravian Church in Jamaica and
the Missionary Church Association in Jamaica

———— ● ◆ ● ————

Congratulations Linley on your insightful presentation of these verses. In these challenging times worldwide, it is most comforting to reflect on domestic events and experiences of years gone by. I recommend this effort as a must read for those who cherish fond memories, and an inspiration for those who look forward to crafting a future of ongoing peace.

Horton Dolphin,
Former Housemaster,
Spanish Teacher and Cricket Coach,
Munro College, 1972-1990

"Mango Time and Pudding and Something More" is a refreshing and interesting anthology that reflects a different, more gentle, civil Jamaica. Throughout his work, you see the love and respect Linley had for his grandparents, parents, and sisters. It explains the values transferred to him through the school system, working in tandem with values he gained at home. It was a simple but fulfilling life. It was a Jamaican way of life.

I submit that Linley has created an opening for some interesting themes for "get togethers." Hit the reset button, put down IG and Tik Tok and come learn something. Eat ah piece of puddin, wash it down with lemonade. "Mango Time, Pudding and Something More" much, much more!

Carolyn Hayle, PhD
C-Level Corporate Executive

History comes alive in vivid scenes of the 60s, 70s and beyond. There is so much that our young people can learn from the plethora of experiences described in "Mango Time, Pudding and Something More".

This book is a must read for everyone who wants to learn about Jamaica of yester year. Heartiest congratulations Linley for sharing with us this inspiring addition to the growing genre of Jamaican Literature.

Sharon Reid,
Retired Principal,
St. Andrew High School for Girls
and Hampton Old Girl

MANGO TIME,
PUDDING

AND SOMETHING MORE

MANGO TIME, PUDDING

AND SOMETHING MORE

POETIC REFLECTIONS ON LIFE IN
WESTERN JAMAICA

LINLEY REYNOLDS

BambuSparks
Kingston, Jamaica, W.I

First printed April 2024

Published by:

BambuSparks Publishing
4 Rochester Avenue,
Kingston 8, Jamaica W.I.
www.bambusparks.com

Cover Design: M.A Rehman

Images are generated by Midjourney and some by the author

Contact the author at ldrconsults@gmail.com to provide feedback or make bulk orders.

A tribute to Mum

PREFACE

This book was written in honour of my beloved Mum, Mrs Violet Reynolds, who poured incessantly into my childhood development. Consequently, the poem 'It's a Beautiful Day' was authored for her thanksgiving service. It was subsequently modified and entitled 'It's a Wonderful Day', to be captured in my next book. She was my main primary school teacher who tirelessly tutored me both at home and at school. Even throughout my adulthood, she was my teacher. Her tutoring is indelibly etched in my mind and I am indeed very grateful for her support throughout my life and would have loved it if she were around to read these poems that I have written.

Her long and busy days as a Vice Principal and then Principal of primary schools, as well as being a wife and a mother, represented a very hectic period of her life. Mum spent in excess of 40 years in the classroom with the majority of those years as a Principal. Her parents were among the members of the working class who lived in western Jamaica. They were disciplined individuals who had a strong belief in a sound work ethic, the benefits of education, albeit attaining minimal levels, and an unwavering commitment to Christ.

Mum's Dad, in his final decades of life, assumed the profession of farmer. His focus was sugarcane and to a lesser extent cattle rearing and mixed vegetable farming. He was highly respected in his community, a local church leader who helped many in various ways for which they were grateful. Her Mum (my grandmother) managed the home with distinction and diligence. She was the epitome of an excellent wife who supported her husband and excelled as a mother and grandmother.

Mum was the second of four daughters for my grandparents. All were encouraged to focus on academics and individually had various successes. Mum's academic achievements peaked at the Moneague College where she successfully completed her Teacher Training Programme. Mum was passionate about teaching and sought to assist as many children as was humanly possible. It was sheer joy for her when Common Entrance Examination results were published in *The Gleaner* (the daily national newspaper), as she wanted to learn of her students who were successful and moving on to high school. Realising her academic prowess, she also had her personal aspirations and sought to blend all aspects of her life which over time proved challenging. Her love for her family soon took precedence. Her commitment to her parents was unshakeable and likewise to her siblings. At all times, she placed Christ at the forefront of her life and made it a point of duty to undertake mission activities.

On January 17, 2023, Mum was called home. Without knowing of her death, I had an epiphany which I started to document. Moments thereafter, I received the call from her doctor who stated that Mum has "been arrested". At that moment I asked, "Has she died?" to which he replied, "Yes." Afterwards I started documenting some specific and special moments in Mum's life as well as the lives of my siblings and I, and this book in the main encapsulates those special moments.

Spending the majority of our childhood in Westmoreland, we had the benefit and support of our extended family which included grandparents, aunts, uncles, and cousins. Communities were closely knit, particularly those in Grange Hill where my grandparents (Mum's Parents) lived and Negril Hills where my Dad's roots were deeply entrenched. My Dad's mother was truly an entrepreneur whose expertise revolved around mixed farming from which she successfully raised her children. Such mixed farming included cattle and horse rearing, tobacco, vegetable farming, coconut and ground provisions. Her large water tank built from cut stone and a pond on the farm provided water for the community.

The poems written in this book represent my perspective, that of my siblings and my family during the late 1960s and 1970s. The poems reflect the post-independence period in Jamaica. This was also a period when sugarcane was king in Westmoreland and when West Indies Sugar Company (WISCO) managed the majority of the farms and was solely responsible for sugar manufacturing in Westmoreland. WISCO was a company wholly owned by the Government of Jamaica. Sugarcane was the mainstay of the economy that resulted in various economic spinoffs in the service industry and throughout the parish.

The stability of many families was directly attributable to the then thriving sugar industry. With the arrangement between Britain and Jamaica, there was always a buyer for all the sugar manufactured in Jamaica. Subsequently, there was the development of the bauxite industry in the adjoining parish of St Elizabeth, which attracted human resources from

Westmoreland. This was a good thing as it created employment and higher remuneration. There was, however, the impact on families, specifically, the families of those who needed to travel long distances daily to work. Our family got caught in this vicious cycle and relocated to ensure reduced travel time to work for Dad as he worked with Alumina Partners of Jamaica (Alpart) in Nain, St Elizabeth during 1970 and beyond.

In 1973, Mum opted to take on this relocation challenge and was successful in her application to become the Principal of Clapham All Age School in deep rural St Elizabeth. This was after planting deep roots at New Hope Primary School in Culloden, Westmoreland. Mum's spirit of compromise and the advancement of family took precedence over her own personal desires and objectives. This assignment gravely troubled her children, who saw the move as retrograde given the rural location, lack of running water and electricity and definitely a slower pace of living. Spending holidays in Grange Hill, Westmoreland with our grandparents was deemed a better alternative than staying in the forested greens of Brighton, St Elizabeth.

Given the benefit of excellent teachers, my siblings and I successfully concluded the Common Entrance Examinations which permitted us to advance to reputable high schools to pursue secondary education. For me, I went to Munro College

– A city set upon a hill cannot be hid. It was a different experience of teaching, learning, meeting other boys from different socio-economic backgrounds, and just being submerged in the culture of Munro. Five decades after entry to Munro College, friendships among many of us who started together remain intact. So deep are the bonds of friendship among boys who went to the College. A segment of this book focuses on life at Munro College.

As most of these poems were written, they brought back fun memories to my siblings and I. Importantly, also, they gave greater insight into my family structure and my boyhood life that my wife and children learnt about and appreciated. Taking them to the various communities where we lived also assisted them in understanding community living and the dynamics between community members. The Christian heritage that was established by my Grandad was a legacy of invaluable worth passed on through generations. We firmly believe that the benefits our family reaped were attributable to the blessings passing down from one generation to the next and the individual belief in Christ that we espouse.

As you read this anthology, it is my fervent desire that the importance of the extended family is realised and as a nation we seek to reinforce the importance of the community in the development of our children. It is also important for extended family members to seek to be good role models for our children. We experienced this with my grandparents and other family members. There was a high level of ethics that undergirded them while pursuing their life's calling. They held on to those important tenets despite the influence of change that was sweeping Jamaica, and which was very evident in Westmoreland.

Note also how children engaged each other and utilised time in group activities that aided in their development. The playing of marbles and gigs or even flying a kite were some of the high points in the lives of many children, specifically boys. Outdoor activities were encouraged and pursued daily. As a family from the poorer class, farming also created a viable option to utilise a young boy's energy in a meaningful manner.

Jamaica today has many people like my siblings and I. However, many of the things we did are now in the distant past, as development and postmodernism have eliminated those activities. This book seeks to recapture some of those activities and experiences we had as children and as a family. The New Market flood, for example, was a catastrophe of unimaginable proportions, which literally covered the town and its environs. Whilst lives were lost, the community, with limited resources and without warning, did exceptionally well in limiting the loss of lives. Commendations are in order for the hardworking community members, local and national government agencies, and USAID of the day for the support extended and the resilience of the locals.

There is also a final point to be made. As we reflect on what was; our favourite persons, our pets and even familiar and favourite places, things have all changed. The house of precious memories is no longer there. The persons we loved have transitioned. We too have changed with the passage of time and the various activities that have impacted us, for better or for worse. Consequently, we must look ahead as life's changes are constant and that is what can be very difficult for most persons. But importantly, and understand this, life moves on for all. Capture the essence of decent, good and Christ-centred living that will create pleasant memories and a meaningful history for generations to come.

I trust that, as you read the poems, they will inspire you and give you a glimpse of beautiful Jamaica in the late 1960s and throughout the 1970s. Hopefully it will inspire and positively impact our younger generation as they navigate a difficult world and look to us the older generation to assist in guiding them.

ACKNOWLEDGMENTS

This anthology came about purely through me documenting an epiphany that I experienced just moments before being advised of the passing of my Mum – Mrs Violet Reynolds.

To my wife, Eileen Diana, who has been extremely patient and supportive, and who believes in my abilities and encouraged me all the way. Even during the days when I was deep in thought and trying to work through the various pieces, I could hear her voice of encouragement.

To Mrs. Alicia Weller, my appreciation for your insight and editorial skills. Also, my children, siblings and extended family members who graciously provided feedback and encouragement.

Importantly, the hand of Almighty God cannot be ignored as it is through Him that I received this ability, now turned talent, which I deeply acknowledge and appreciate.

CONTENTS

The Foundation of a Resilient Family

Our extended family – The display of love, commitment and resilience and excellent work ethics

1 - Home of Homes

Small board house of little note, not much different from neighbour's abode.

The style and layout of general mode, pitched on blocks which bore the load,

Two feet above ground the standard code,

Little cosy veranda, like a central node.

Light brown clinker board, smooth and polished,

Used to build this house so small and modest.

Glowing coloured oil paint, sand dash finished.

Internally the colours are no less diminished.

Distinctive in colour and reflective of spirit,

Such a lovely little home we would visit,

Our kind and loving grandparents lived in it.

Kitchen and latrine outside and apart,

Access in the night required a brave heart,

Through the darkness you wished you could dart,

Be careful of a frog that may cross your path.

Good ole faithful *chamber pot*,

Carefully used and returned to the spot.

Targeted aim, required a straight shot.

Nightly use, required little thought,

Make every effort, everything is caught.

Washing it was the first chore of the morning,

After nightly use there should be no scorning.

Cleansed with soap and water, it was spotless white.

Dried by the morning sun, awaiting the night.

Guttered water we regularly received, piped water so
frequently deceived.

Drums and pans we constantly refilled, water conservation was
always instilled.

Kitchen was a favourite place for all, where we waited for the meal's call.

Small wooden benches twelve inches tall, provided such comfort as the minutes crawl.

From the kerosene stove there was smoke, far less than the wood fire we had to stoke.

Grandma skillfully managed the fire, her expertise one would easily desire.

Complete and tasty meals she prepared, generous servings she always shared.

Her culinary skills beyond compare, reflected her heart, full of love and care.

Inside this little house we all convened, Grandma petite was distinctly queen.

Lanky Grandpa, his Bible he'd read, family devotions he'd diligently lead.

Everyone should pray, was his nightly plea, all should be done before the night's tea.

Neighbours on the left and neighbours on the right,

Their colourful speech we listened to with delight.

With little distracting noises we clearly heard,

All their secrets, no one stopped nor the other deterred.

Cats, dogs and chickens were kept, on the almond tree the chickens slept.

In the house you'll always see the cat, comfortably curled on her favourite mat.

Elf the dog led the pack, loving the front yard, but slept in the back.

Home of homes we all loved, with grandparents, our beloved.

Small board house of little note, the grandest of homes we'd all vote.

Size and colour of no issue; a place of solace, or rescue.

Many times conversations ensued, love and passion of teenagers imbued.

The fun and laughter that filled our play was the fire that lit and energised our day.

2 - Demeanour So Calming

Grandma, short and petite, was wonderfully made complete.

Cocoa brown hue, grandpa being her beau.

With her long, thick, black hair, Harry her husband dear.

Having minimal education, was good at communication.

Woman of the soil, unafraid to toil.

Cooking, washing, ironing, or cleaning, was always bright and beaming.

The strength she had, came from God, on whom she was always leaning.

Dedicated to her family; was fearful of calamities.

Chicken merry, hawk draw near, her warning used to scare.

Market day was a busy day which started dark and early.

Home Sweet Home accompanied her lady, from bedroom, hall, and scullery.

Breakfast she did, was a quick fix, for Harry to leave by six.

On her knee, her wooden floor to clean, which always had a sheen.

Coconut brush and Rexo floor polish were items used to astonish.

Onto market she went, this was her Friday's drill,

From the district of Geneva to the town called Grange Hill.

Other housewives she would greet, no time to stop and meet.

A quick hello or how do you do, the salutation she would repeat.

Marketplace her focus, likewise, the beef stall.

In she went, crowded and noisy, to her favourite vendors, all.

Ground provisions from the stall, then came the vendor's call.

Learning of the pricey vegetables she advanced but with a crawl.

With a successful morning at the market, on her head she places her basket.

A full basket on her head, which includes a loaf of bread.

Now her trek home commences, her basket she masterly balances.

With many years of experience, her skill is like a science.

Weekly to the market she goes without showing defiance.

Thirty minutes of walking home, with no time to roam.

Friday evening pumpkin soup, a favourite, her family eagerly awaits.

With provisions, dumplings, and beef from the butcher's weights.

Three pounds of pumpkin for her soup, all enjoyed, to the very last scoop.

Everyone received their portion, belly full and in distortion.

What a lengthy and busy Friday morning, she conquered with a demeanour so calming.

3 - Bottles of Glass

So early in the mornings, yet Grandma would rise.

Brewing her pot of chocolate, was there any surprise?

Cooking saltfish and green bananas, soft and nice.

Spongy light brown johnny cakes, always served twice.

For the hard work ahead, this meal would suffice.

Having patched the holey tyre now it's time; we both must go.

Grandpa mounts the worn bicycle, expertly riding, albeit slow.

Onto the crossbar grandson sits, enduring the tow.

Gradual acceleration as we went, riding on the main road;

Riding daily, rain or shine, was generally the mode.

To the farm we must go, at times with a load.

Come let's view the patch, where seeds were recently sown.

Look how quickly they have burst, seedlings all have grown.

Yam is dug, what a weighty tuber, firm and dark brown.

An arduous task it was, done without a groan.

Yet there's more work to be done before tools are down.

Yards away are cows, chewing the long green grass.

Patiently they are waiting; to the milk stall at last.

Now the milk is collected, in bottles of glass.

All must be preserved, none should be lost.

Milk is so fresh and nice, to others there's a cost.

On the other side of the fence, was a bull, full and stern.

Untie the rope, give him a jerk, hold him strong and firm.

What an obedient bull, responsive to the pull.

Unaware of its quick steps, as the bull briskly treks.

Frightened out of his wits, with no time to delay.

Dropping the rope and a quick dash, seemed the only way.

So quick was the bull, its speed now on display.

In the background he shouted, Grandpa was far away.

Work is over, both so tired, can we make it home?

A crocus bag with provisions, from the fertile loam.

On our back it goes, the weight we do not know.

Walking down the hill, satisfied and slow.

Just a glimpse of the bull, in my mind it stayed.

Onto the bicycle once again, riding on the plain.

Safely reaching home, the bags we unlade.

There waiting for us was a wife and grandmother.

Drop those dirty clothes, tomorrow there's another.

Thanking God for a hard day's work from which we did not hide.

Just a glimpse of the bull was always on my mind.

For health and strength Grandpa prayed, and daily for His lead.

For his family to feed, and to meet their daily needs.

Opulence was never desired, so fearful of greed.

But what an energetic bull, so full of speed.

4 - Aunt Maud

Letter she wrote to her parents.
They already knew of her talents.
Strong and resilient with no match.
She did her work with great dispatch.

Confused and shocked at the contents,
Looking at his wife and then he laments.
My elegant first daughter is terminally ill.
Lord, in your presence I remain still.

When will we see our daughter again,
As composure they both sought to regain.
A quick response by way of a letter,
As they prayed for her to get better.

Not more than two years was she given,
Would not deter her spirit for living.

A visit to Jamaica to see family and friends,
Her love and gifts she extends.

So quickly her vacation has ended,
Her love for parents and family validated.
Her sorrowful parents contemplated,
When next their daughter they'll see.
Don't you both worry for me.
Let's go to the kitchen and have some tea.
Pray to God, that was her plea.

Month by month her letters she'd write.
Every letter received, to her parents' delight.
Her condition was no longer a plight.
As her medical care seemingly was right,
Extended her life now looking so bright.

Thirty years on and she seemed strong,
Life is good and indeed prolonged.
Removing from her life all that's wrong,
And every day on, finding a song.
Resilient and focused, keeping calm.
God her keeper, remained her balm.

5 - Aunt Em

Holiday time and the children were excited.

Family get-togethers, all would be invited.

Visiting grandparents, where we're all heading.

Just vacationing with them was always appealing.

School books left; none this trip were taken.

Their weight and size, my bag would be laden.

On the other hand, fun and laughter will not be forsaken.

A letter from Miss Em was all Grandma wanted.

Therein her arrival date would be stated.

Travelling on Mr Ribby's crowded Ford minibus,

From Kingston to Grange Hill at the terminus.

What a journey on treacherous roads, the driver was so cautious.

Travelling one hundred and twenty miles was a hectic ride.

Looking down the road, Miss Em now makes her strides.

All full of smiles: finally she arrives.
A long day's journey, it's now past five.
Nothing else but bed as she revives.
Next day's approaching and time to jive.

Miss Em was a primary school teacher,
She was their third daughter,
Was always full of laughter.
It didn't matter what time you caught her,
Bright eyes and smile was her demeanour.

At evening times, the community we'd walk.
Aunt Em greeting and doing all the talk.
"This is my nephew and here are my nieces,
Holiday with aunt and grands is what pleases,
They love fun and enjoy my teases."

The next day, to the matinee we'd go,
To watch the afternoon's feature show.
Nothing less than fine comedy.
Like Popeye and Olive, His Fair Lady.

But what fun it was walking into town,
With our Aunt Em who was well-known.
People exclaimed, what a way the children have grown,

All that one, she's slim and brown.

"All of them are Miss Harry's own."

Was Aunt Em's retort, all should've known.

Returning home, we stopped by Maas Clar.

His shop at Geneva Crossing had a small bar.

We are just enquiring how you are?

My Aunt as she spoke to Maas Clar.

Across the road was Miss Ruth's shop,

Always opened, having little stock.

Wherever we went we stopped and talked.

This is how it was, in the community we walked.

Music blaring and people gathering,

Holiday time while some are staggering.

A fun-filled time it ought to be.

People bright and chatty, full of glee.

Enjoying the coming together, in bright tropical weather.

Despite the hardships which don't seem a bother,

People all together for some fun and laughter,

With our Aunt Em, who made it brighter.

6 - Aunt Ter

Enquiring mind of a growing boy,
Confined in the house brought him little joy.
Probing outdoors instead of playing with toys,
Made him feel better and his life enjoy.

This Saturday morning was no different from any,
Going outside felt somewhat uncanny.
Through the yard he went, in his familiar spaces,
As if going through his routines and paces.
There in front was a small brown tree limb.
Crushing it seemed normal to him.

What a piercing pain it was,
In a split second through the shoe the nail went.
Crumpled on the ground he bent,
Cries and screams of discontent.
In minutes to the hospital, he was sent.

You must get an injection to prevent an infection.

Oh no, this will cause contention,

As his only position was dissension.

Well, send for my Aunt Ter, was his confession.

His well-being was her single intention.

His Aunt Ter was a registered nurse.

Soft and genteel, easy to converse.

Giving the injection she couldn't reverse.

Accepting the injection, she'll need to coerce.

"Don't make it hurt Aunt Ter," was his response.

A rub and a squeeze and a little tease,

In a few quick moments the injection she released.

Oh what pain it was, has not left his mind.

Hasn't changed his views, his Aunt Ter was kind.

Visiting her at the hospital gave such delight.

Her compassionate demeanour made patients bright.

Spotless white uniform and a cap so daintily perched,

Gave her access and the requisite right as she nursed.

What a spectacle it was, her riding to work.

The exercise she got was a very good perk.

Through Savanna-la-Mar town she rode.

Everyone saw her on the road.

Admired her commitment and mode,

Bright white uniform was the single code.

With over 40 years of nursing,

She showed no shirking.

Daily walking through the wards,

Attending patients and updating records.

Her expertise and skills her family needed,

Not just for medicine but for meals she created.

Her breakfast, lunch and dinner,

Was always a winner.

For everyone who tasted, the next meal they'll be eager.

Her energetic son, onto the roads he went,

Ignoring instructions, his Mum had set.

Whilst lashing her son, he always pleaded,

Mum I've learnt and have heeded.

No more trouble I'll give, he conceded.

The following day, his pleas erased,

Back on the roads, his steps retraced.

On becoming a seasoned midwife,

She helped to prevent the surgeon's knife.

She assisted birthing mothers,

To manage pain so rife,

In anticipation of a new life.

Achieving the level of Sister,

No one tried to diss her.

Rising through the ranks to Matron,

Was never ever a straight run.

Her experience and knowledge caused some to be miffed,

Not realising it came through long days she worked on shifts.

Her elderly parents she always attended,

For their medicines, on her they depended.

Helping many, she was always commended,

For her outreach, deliberate and intended.

Service beyond self is what transcended.

A nurse for all, of no comparison they contended.

7 - Memories of Negril Hills

Listen carefully, are the birds chirping?

Listen, from a distance the rooster is crowing,

Hens with chickens are they clucking?

Home Sweet Home provides Grandma with lighting,

Look around and you see the morning is dawning.

Negril Hills where Granny Edna lives; a new day is coming.

What an aroma throughout the house.

Local coffee is brewing and tantalising my senses,

Preparing breakfast, Granny Edna commences.

Cows bracing the wooden fences.

Frivolous calves, the dogs they incense,
As their playing becomes intense.

Soon the horses are brought to the stall.
Schoolboy, the horse, answered my call.
Blinkers and saddles were fitted on all,
Reining them in, to the riders they submitted.
The pastures they'd go, for which they're committed.
Riders all, it's a long day ahead they admitted.
As milking cows, what an arduous chore they repeated.

The frosty morning, under the covers I love.
The sun piercing through, warmth from above.
A day on the farm, there's so much to do.
I'd rather sit on the veranda looking at the view.
A neighbour is passing by, little boy is that you?
In his thick dungaree all in blue.

Lush green vegetation, what a lovely hue,
Of the trees and shrubs that hold the clue.
Too young to sip that tantalising brew,
Here's your breakfast grandson, especially for you.
Home grown cocoa making your tea,
Cow's milk and brown sugar added you'll see.
Strength for the day, all would agree.

In a thick aluminium pan, to the condensery the milk goes,

Looking at vegetables as they started to grow.

A bull kin to the butcher we had to show.

So much work on the farm, did you know?

Staying home in the cosy bed you'd agree,

No support I'd get, even with a plea.

Success through hard work, the only guarantee.

Further yet, hard work for boys was the decree.

Attending the farm animals brought joy to me.

Walking through the farm, feeling free.

Drinking a jelly coconut was sweeter than tea.

Farm work so hard, may surpass a degree.

The accomplishments are there for all to see.

Childhood Experiences and Family Happenings

Activities at home and curiosity as life unfolded

8 - Four Little Children

Roosters crowing and birds chirping,
Noisy birds disturbing my dreaming.
Here comes Mum intense and screaming,
Wake up children, it's a school morning.
Within thirty minutes we are all leaving.
Cold water shower for my bathing,
That morn's task I shall be waiving.

Hear Dad shouts, "The car is not starting.
Children, please come and give the car a push."
As he yelled, then Mum said, "hush,
Neighbours sleeping don't disturb them."
Sonny started coughing, he has phlegm,
Pet's gown is torn, requiring a hem.
Jackie is outside feeding the hens,
Sharon is now looking for her pen.

Turning, turning, the car isn't starting,
One two three; push as hard as you can.
Four little children, weak and frail,
Pushing no faster than a slug or snail.

Faster, faster, Dad started yelling.
Four little children doing their best.
This exercise is a very hard test;
Push and push, now needing to rest.

Faster, faster, Dad was still yelling;
Onto the road for all to see.
Four little children without tea.
Neighbours laughing so full of glee.

Buying a car gave us status,
Nothing more shameful, they're laughing at us.
Help us, Lord, to keep our focus,
That neighbours' perception will in no way shape us.

9 - Here Comes December

Here comes December, one to remember.

Anxious men and women all in a wonder.

Cutting sugar cane caused them to ponder,

Hard work it was, nothing else but labour.

The heavens overcast, working thereunder.

Mum's intense belly pains, now in a slumber.

Doctor confirms, she's now in labour.

Here comes Dad calling calling.

Why such a visit so early in the morning?

Grandma and Grandpa eager to know,

Jumped from their beds and went to the door.

Opened the front door and let him in.

The still of the morning, so dark and dim.

Here comes Dad calling calling.

Men dressed and ready, gathered in the dark.

Waiting to commence their hard day's work.

Cutting sugarcane, they did not shirk.

Dad seemed so bright, none dared to ask.

What was the news and why did he bask?

Here comes Dad calling calling.

Mum had a baby; it is a pretty girl.

Everyone heard and did a little swirl.

Then he said, she is my Pearl.

There on her head was a single curl.

Here comes Dad calling calling.

Four little girls and one little boy.

Sisters teasing their sorrowful brother,

And so he said, Mum will have another.

Doctor's orders you are done.

One little boy remains your only son.

Here comes Dad calling calling.
This little baby girl grew up so quickly.
Bird-like voice will she be a singer?
In her youth she acted like a doctor.
Her patient then, was her only brother.

Here comes her brother calling calling.
Patient is ill, and in need of food.
A thick slice of bread for him to chew,
Glass like a silo all filled with milo.
This did the trick and gave away the clue.

Here comes Dad calling calling.
This little girl is now fully grown.
Singer or doctor who will know.
Full of talent for her to own.

Leaving school dressed in her gown.
Telling everyone her future she'll own,
No matter what, it's looking bright.
Lead her dear God as you're the light.
In all her decisions that they'll be right.

10 - Our Favourite Dog

Little puppy given to us as a gift,
Full of energy, he was so swift.
Coloured white and spotted brown,
With time he became fully grown.
Prince, our dog, obedient to the core,
Was always willing to explore.

Little puppy given to us as a gift.
As he ran, he did a quick shift,
As he grew, he was crowned king.

None could withstand him in the ring.

There was love that he was shown.

He always disliked being alone.

Little puppy given to us as a gift.

Now a weighty dog you wouldn't lift.

Rain and lightning was his scare,

Under the bed to hide his fear.

Little puppy given to us as a gift.

I'm telling you don't come near,

A thunderous bark for all to hear.

As the family to him was always dear.

Little puppy given to us as a gift.

Show me the chicken if you dare,

I'll catch it for your care.

No harm, I'll do it if instructions are clear.

This puppy, a dog oh so rare,

All we wanted was for him to be near.

Little puppy given to us as a gift.

There was war on rodents all,

'Rat, Prince, rat' was the urgent plea.

At the flash of light he was full of glee.

Job well done now it's time for a meal,
Cornmeal and chicken back was the deal.

Little puppy given to us as a gift.
Morning dawning, he came calling.
Swimming time, he was bawling,
"Get up *Vie*! I'll take you hauling."
Rain or breeze, he rode the wave,
Nothing could stop him from this rave.

Little puppy given to us as a gift.
Age and stage, no more could he rage.
Still, you had a spirit so dear.
Once again, a canine rare.
Wearing his crown in dog heaven
Our favourite dog beyond comparison.

11 - Fifteen Minutes

Fifteen minutes swim in the Caribbean Sea,
Was all I needed with my tea.
Accompanied by my canine dear,
Was one of a kind, oh so rare.

Fifteen minutes swim in the Caribbean Sea,
That's all I asked, was my plea.
White and spotted was his hue,
His own objective was the blue.

Fifteen minutes swim in the Caribbean Sea,

Was for two and not for three.

The freshness of the water was so calming,

Causing anticipation, the new day's dawning.

Fifteen minutes swim in the Caribbean Sea,

Look beyond and what did I see.

A ship sailing on the silvery horizon,

A fisherman's boat of little comparison.

Either vision of peaceful view reminded me there's work to
do.

Fifteen minutes swim in the Caribbean Sea,

Not much longer can I stay, students, all are on their way.

Restraining my desire, my focus now is on the hire.

Parents to meet, students to greet.

Minds so bright, help me Lord to shed some light.

12 - Beat with a Nod

Under the eaves of the house, they all are nestled.

Moving around in limited space as if they wrestled.

So many of them, all upside down.

Similar in size, and colour being brown.

Fluttering wings, it appeared they all had,

Moving around seemingly to a beat with a nod.

Don't trouble us, and we won't attack you.

If you trouble us, stings await, you never knew.

Was never enough to cause him any fear.

Down with the nest, it can't stay there.

Was the decision, he thought, was clear.

Pondering the task at hand, he had to be quick.

Searching the yard, he found a long and slender stick.

With a swift prick at the nest, it surely would be down.

But only one attempt to hit it to the ground.

This little boy pondered each step in his mind,

As all the processes had to be aligned.

His escape route was all very clear,

Running so fast as cutting through air.

Nonstop you must go, until all is clear.

Any stop you make, stings you must bear.

But when do you stop, when is it all clear?

He could not say as that was unclear.

All he knew was his speed was fast and rare.

No one ever caught him, a race they wouldn't dare.

Satisfied with his plan, it's time for action.

Reviewing the process, no time for protraction.

With the stick held high, a show of intention.

Ensuring a perfect aim and quick hand action.

Hitting his target, he sped off, what a quick reaction!

Unto his escape route as he bent,

Adrenaline released he was sent,

Full of speed and in ascent,

Propelled him so fast as he went.

But behind him were cries, which he feared.
The strategy he planned was not shared,
With his sister for whom he cared,
Stung by the wasps whom he dared.

Quickly he went to her rescue.
It shouldn't be me, but you,
Was her shouting while she cried.
Not much running she even tried,
If only she had watched and followed,
Now on the ground she wallowed.
Indeed remorseful, and now he sorrowed.

How can I explain this to our parents?
A real challenge this presents.
I can hear Dad arguing, ignoring my brilliance,
Calling it nothing but youthful exuberance.
My tolerance and bravery now seemed unsavoury.
Sharon my sister, with swells and pains,
Did not interfere, but those were her gains.

13 - A Coloured Kite

As the breeze blew, he got so excited,
Wondering if friends will join, if invited.
Is this the right time for flying a kite?
Will the breeze get stronger, or will it stop?
Do I have enough kite paper in my stock?
Will I have time to go to the shop?
So many questions, but I won't stop.

Kite paper, paste and bamboo strips,
To the shop he must quickly make a trip.
Getting some items to make his kite hip.

Bright kite paper of various colours,
The kite he'll make will be multicoloured.

Quickly he went about framing the kite.
Bamboo strips tied firm and tight.
Overlayed with thin coloured paper bright.
Now a lovely kite that is large and light.

Outside we went with this coloured kite.
Jackie patiently held it in the air.
Stand by, don't move, wait right there.
As he stepped away, the cord to bear.
A gust of breeze and the kite she released.
Ten feet high it briskly reached.

Running down the yard,
Releasing more cord.
Soon the kite sang, making a chord.
More cord it got, the greater the bent.
As if at the centre, there was dissent.

Further and further, away the kite goes.
Everyone watched as if it was a show.
Look at the kite swaying right to left,
Leveraging the cord, reflecting deft.

Suddenly, the kite came to a halt.

Impossible! we shouted; how did it stall?

Was there an invisible hand that held it still?

Everyone watching as this was a thrill.

As the gentle breeze blew, the display of skill.

Again, the kite started swaying.

Look, is the slender tail fraying?

This time it goes from left to right,

Then as it goes, gaining further height,

Further it ascends, as on a flight.

What a wonderful afternoon, all were saying.

Flying the coloured kite was so satisfying.

Making it was equally gratifying.

Not having enough coloured paper he abhors.

Being prepared and ready, he implores.

Waiting on a gust of wind, that will come for sure.

Flying a kite was fun, boys loved and wanted more.

14 - Almost a Tear

Little boy left his home without permission.

On his way he undertook a mission.

Raising birds as pets was his vision.

What would his parents think; his admission.

With much self-reasoning he took a decision.

Whatever their thoughts, for him there was no indecision.

Can I hold one of your birds, the little boy asked?
Will it peck or should I wear a mask?
With such excitement the little boy laughed.
Seemed like holding the bird was a big task.
What a moment it was holding the bird at last.

So soft, smooth and calm it was.
Not a flutter or movement or even a buzz.
No flapping of wings to cause any fuss.
Bright-eyed bird, a lovely sight it was.

The colour of the bird was soft and soothing.
Black ringed neck and plumage light brown.
With a similar colour on its crown,
Were they ever at the pet shop in town?
Not to worry anymore, a pair I'll own.

No money to make a dollar or even to spare,
How can I convince him I do care?
Sir, your birds are lovely, can I buy a pair?
Show me your money, as these birds are rare.
Sad and desperate with almost a tear,
At that moment to God I whispered a prayer.

Small holey brown box he gave the little boy.

Here you are, a pair of Barbary doves,

Praying dear God, the birds his Dad will love,

Home bound he went, with his pair of Barbary doves.

Under his bed the boy thought was safe.

For the cat they surely would appease.

A lovely meal, if you ever dear to please.

No way was it his desire, the cat to please or tease.

So he kept watching, he wasn't at ease.

At long last Dad came through the gate.

The question he thought, what was Dad's state?

Happy or sad, the boy could not wait.

Dad he shouted, don't be in a rage,

As I have pets needing a cage.

Dad rubbed his head and stood in a daze.

Then at his son he looked with a long gaze.

Son, your birds are lovely, we will raise.

Dad left the room to build a cage with haste.

Jubilant and happy the little boy ran in a maze.

Let's go to the feedstore to get some maize.

Early in the mornings a song or two they sang.

It was on time like the bell the teacher rang.

Time to rise for the chores must be done.

When you're finished to me you must come.

My water and grain I will need.

As you know I love my seeds.

Discipline and order the doves all preached.

All as they multiplied, a dozen they had reached.

15 - A Catch Awaits

Rising early as the new day is dawning.

The freshness of the air is always so calming.

His outstretched arms way above his head,

Get the wrinkles out of your eyes, out of bed.

Those were the words that Dad boldly said.

Get up son, let's go fishing right away.

A request so strange, it's a work day.

The fishing line and bait Dad swiftly grabbed.

Behind him his little boy walked and lagged.
Two minutes' walk now by the sea,
What a peaceful view for all to see.

Unto the hook he promptly placed the bait,
Wishing for a swift catch to shorten the wait.
Early in the mornings the catch should be great.
Pondering his thoughts, he must leave by eight.

Wondering in which direction a catch or two awaits.
Fishing requires patience, he quietly states.
Effortlessly he swirls the blue line around,
Releasing the line, going where it is bound.
Sitting on the rock Dad patiently is waiting,
A seagull flies by the area it is stalking.
Jerking the line intermittently he tries,
Is there a catch, or a fish's demise?

Minutes went by and a jerk Dad makes.
The line is so firm, for fear it breaks.
Pull and a pull, no further chance he'll take.
Wading through the water is a risky stake.
Be careful Dad, my heart starts to ache.
Stop pulling the line, gently give a shake.

Out of the sea, wondering what held the hook.

Looking at his son, his instructions he took.

Wondering, his insight, was it from a book?

Not to worry anymore, the release of the hook.

With seaweed and cloudy water, he couldn't look.

Dad surmised a rock was there that caught the hook.

Throwing back the line in the very same spot,

Would the outcome differ, he's wondering not.

This was the decision he thought he wisely took.

Curious to understand what really held the hook.

A few moments later and after a jerk,

The line was so stiff, Dad went berserk.

Come on little son let's pull in the line,

Something is funny, I'm scared this time.

Pull and pull yet no release.

Let's continue Dad, no time to cease.

A final pull and there comes the ease.

A dangling feeling is that what it seems?

Reeling in the line, as fast as we could.

Something is there, is that really good?

Anxious two, the line we reeled in.
Is it a big fish resisting the catch?
Son and father together, with strength to match,
Kept reeling in, soon the catch we'll watch.

Wow! Look at it, deep orange in colour.
Dad this is astonishing, we displayed valour.
Tentacles frantically moving all around.
An octopus so large, let's put it on the ground.

Never before an octopus we caught,
Preparing the catch from instructions we sought.
Seasoning the pot as Mum had taught.
A dinner for our cat, so rare we thought.

Early morning fishing was always fun.
Catching an octopus, in the rising sun.
Wasn't the idea of fishing for his son.
What surprise it was, together we were stunned
Understanding the challenge, neither would have shunned.

16 - Five Cents

Five cents of any value to anyone around?

At lunchtime, to the shop I'm bound.

Cocoa bread and patty make me feel happy.

Back to school again, no longer feeling snappy.

Five cents of any value to anyone around?

Here comes a pullet on the ground.

Dad says that's the cost of the game;

I can't believe she has become so tame.

Each morning to the door she came,

Getting her grain, her sole aim.

Five cents of any value to anyone around?

Yellow feet, shiny plumage all in brown,

Distinctive bright red comb was her glowing crown.

Walking stealthily through the bushes down,

Days pass, she's nowhere to be found.

Searching thickets, a dozen eggs on the mound.

I can't believe she has laid them brown!

Five cents of any value to anyone around?

Here she comes now vexed and moody,

I can't understand the change so snooty.

Only thereafter I learnt she's broody.

Outstretched wings as if attacked,

A dozen chicks she has hatched.

Here they come, encircling her feet,

Looking for grain, so they eat.

Five cents of any value to anyone around?

One five cents, now thirteen five cents.

No longer a dissent, for her baby chicks she's a tent.

For her offspring she must fend, once again I'm her friend.

Five cents of any value to anyone around?

What else apart from throwing it on the ground?

Help us Lord to understand its worth,

If you must, permit a rebirth,

To maximise on resources, as we walk this earth.

17 - Deepest Rural Call

Let's go to Cheltenham, Brighton, and Clapham,
Where livestock graze and farmers plant yam.
Up and down we go, boys playing with a ram.
Beautiful, peaceful villages, all little-known.
All fertile grounds, where vegetables are grown.

Deep rural mountainous districts, mostly green.
Chilly morning air was always fresh and clean.
People of the community, all looking keen.
Daily walking to and fro mostly appearing lean.
Mules and donkeys all heavily laden,
Onto the main road to offload their burden.

Chatty school children all were alerted,
Their learning should not be subverted.
Send them all, both big and small,
New principal was found, inducted for them all,
Now undertaking her deepest rural call.

Teachers, parents alike, committed to the cause.
Learning is so important, our children shall not pause.
Children were on time, they got an applause.
Working hard and diligently to eliminate flaws.

Principal's children terribly appalled,
The stillness of the greens they recalled.
There all around were trees standing tall.
So, they screamed and yelled,
As everything was at a crawl.
Let's go back to Culloden where we had it all.
Fixed on their desire, ignorant of her call.

Empty roads and pathways as it came to night.
No electricity to even shed a light.
Moonlit sky brightened the night,
Enlightened pathways and supported sight.
Home Sweet Home was adequately bright,
For completion of homework which must be right.

Be careful with the gauzy *Tilley* lest you cause a plight.

Used in shops and churches where the light must be bright.

Out it goes and the shrewd shopkeeper is unable to complete his tally

Neither would the persistent preacher be able to conclude his rally.

Morning chores you just don't shun,

Feeding the dogs must be done.

Chicken and birds get their grains,

Grassland for goats, even when it rains.

To the milkman you must go, be careful not to *buck* your toe,

For the pathway was slippery and rocky, even the donkey required a good jockey.

Ordinary folks were busy each day, as they had to earn their way.

Everyone found something to do, kept them all from feeling blue.

Carpenter, tailor, mason, farmer, dressmaker all.

Everyone undertook their call, no one shunned or bawled.

Taking the rocky road up, even if at a crawl.

Thanking God for their gift,

As they worked, seemingly, not to drift.

Primary School Days

*Learnings and interactions accompanied
with fun, frolic and laughter.*

18 - Vaccination Day

Protecting the nation's children, all would agree,

From the budget debate there was a decree.

Children to be vaccinated, none shall disagree.

Through each parish the local authorities made their plea.

As uncertain parents embraced a wait and see.

Public health nurses dressed in brown,

Visiting each parish, they are now in town.

Arriving at schools, all in their gowns.

As each child, big or small, must get their own.

To prevent certain diseases even when grown.

Individually, children went to the Principal's office,

Some vexed faces as if keeping malice,

Others smiling as if they got a treat,

Yet there were those that got cold feet.

Teacher I'm sick, can I have a seat?

Shouts and cries, for some, it was very painful.

Some closed their eyes, they seemed very tearful.

Each had their story, immunisation was the aim.

Yet there were those who thought it was a game.

To the bushes scared boys ran to take cover.

Thinking by the end of day everything would be over.

Send the big boys to scour and uncover,

Mounds, trees, and grass all over.

As all must be immunised within the hour.

Soon the boys are all caught,

Pushing and pulling, to the Principal we were brought.

Now boys, this is not what you were taught.

Vaccinations prevent infections, if caught.

You know the right thing, in the classroom there's a chart.

Now you must get your very own,
Follow me to the nurse in brown.
Oh how he started to cower.
Quickly little boy, we'll be done in the hour.

Little boy, the nurse said, while rolling up his sleeve.
Take a deep breath, no need to heave.
Just be calm, as she rubbed his arm.

Look how quickly it's over, now you can leave.
No need to look upset or even peeved.
Give me a smile, you took it in style.

What a traumatising experience it was,
All the hype and the buzz.
Other boys anxious and in a fuss,
Not wanting to talk or even discuss,
Protecting our children is a big plus.

What is that swelling on the arm?
It's the after effect, just be calm.
In a few days it will all be gone
Check your left arm, if there's a scar.
Evidence after many years, yet no harm.

19 - Tiki Tiki Fish

School day ends and now it's time for home.

Mum's clear instructions don't you all roam.

Walking home from school was never resisted,

Better with friends when they accompanied.

A rainy evening was always enjoyed.

With or without raincoats we had fun.

Walking in the puddles, some would have none,

But catching tiki tiki fish, all would have some.

So many tiki tiki fish, amazing you'd think.

Where did they come from almost in a wink.

Some you caught and placed in bottles.

Clearing the road as an engine throttles.

Here comes a van with such velocity,

Tiki tiki fish around causing curiosity.

All splashed and thoroughly drenched,

The school bag we had was tightly clenched.

Yet holding a bottle, with tiki tiki fish in it.

With such haste it came, surpassing the speed limit,

Had me transfixed for more than a minute.

Wondering who could really be driving that van?

Surely he was irresponsible or an angry man.

His poor behaviour we could not withstand,

It didn't matter much, tiki tiki fish was in hand.

What fun it was walking home in the rain,

Nature is alive and an experience to gain.

Mum's heart saddened and terribly in pain,

Children on a frolic, her instructions in vain.

20 - Walking Home from School

Walking home from school was thirty minutes away.

A shop by the school's gate with pastry on display.

Ring cake, cocoa bread or bulla, a penny you'd pay.

Just seeing the pastry was moreish each day.

Passing Barber Lee, was always busy and friendly,

Greeting him his response was so bright and spritely.

Hello mi amigo, he responded so confidently.

Sitting in his chair he attends to you gently.

A pleasant experience it was, he worked so deftly.

Lovely houses you pass while on your way,
Built by successful persons, all well known.
Wondering if in time, one you'd call your own;
Schoolwork the foundation until fully grown.

Look at the focused dogs seemingly knowing their status.
All appear fearless, their thunderous barks scare us.
Active and alert by the gate they stand guard,
Waiting on their master for whom there's regard.

Walking by Torrington Bridge with manicured greens.
Bone white buildings added to the scene.
Where's the bridge they speak of, it's left to be seen.
Such a lovely landscape always looking clean.

Pleasant people and lovely places you would see.
Men laughing by the bar, all full of glee.
Happy housewives gathered, all having tea.
Tell me please, if you can, what my future will be?

21 - Mermaid

No one wanted to disturb their focused approach.

Children in school, behind their desks they crouched,

As the engaged teachers explained and coached,

They showed no sign of discontent or reproach,

As questions they had, they could easily broach.

But soon the bell rang and the quiet was broken.

Most children stood up before the teacher had spoken.

Children, it's break time so 15 minutes are taken.

Some children were so quiet, it seemed they've just woken.

So quickly the children ran outside.

All in groups quietly talking about the general downside.

An area prohibited because it was the pond side,

Seemed fascinating as children ran to the fence but stayed on the inside.

This is where something is strange and now becoming the upside,

For in the mysterious pond large and deep, it is said, the mermaid resides.

Back to classes after a 15-minute break.

Teacher observed, none drank water or even crunched a flake.

'What's happening children, give me an update'.

All were quiet for everyone's sake.

'Not responding is your take but later on, I'll require an update'.

Children started to chat with each other.

Everyone wanted to keep details under cover.

But what if the teacher heard and told mother?

The children agitated but wanted to bond together.

Then a student shouted, "Miss, can you keep a secret?

Promise us you won't speak, Miss, you won't regret."

Quietly, the student whispered in her ear.

With a smile bursting through teacher said, "that's rare!"
Then teacher said, "let's go midday to see what's there."

Suddenly there was excitement in the class,
Waving her finger, regaining order at last.
Tell me students about this mermaid.
In the pond we are told, she abides.
Midday she rises, for air to stay alive,
And to comb her hair, before returning to where she hides.

Teacher's excitement now aroused, secret for all now
espoused.
Twenty minutes to midday and readying to go pondside.
Then the Principal appears, almost wanting to chide.
"Soon it will be exams; let me see your study guide.
Apply yourself; don't allow your curiosity to subside."
Children smiled and nodded and thanked the Principal
For the tips she shared for life in general.

Teacher and students to the pondside they went,
In the bushes they quietly knelt.
At the glistening water they all stared with intent.
So still it was, not a movement, ripple, or indent.
Midday passes and they still waited,
All the children sad and now deflated.

Seemingly despondent, their curiosity now abated.

So quickly they all went back to their classroom.

Let's have lunch, here's a macaroon.

None of the children cared to eat or return outside.

Experience they had, mermaid, an old fable with a downside.

Principal walked by, trying to hide her smile.

Curiosity you must have, but always use some guile.

22 - Bicycle Time

Have you ever thought of riding a bicycle?

Balancing, pedalling, and focusing all at once.

It comes with spills, fun and thrills.

Riding on the plains or up the hills.

Riding a bicycle requires so many skills.

Riding fast or riding slow, be careful how you go.

Teaching a child to ride is best in open spaces.

There's the risk of falling that the child faces.

The trickiest part is balancing the bike,

Cuts and bruises are badges you generally won't like.

It's your certification of skill, in time you'll hype.

Riding fast or riding slow, be careful how you go.

But so much skill is required to do a *standstill*,
Balancing on the bicycle not moving at will.
Boys competing, who could *standstill* the longest,
Only by winning the contest are you the best.

Riding fast or riding slow, be careful how you go

But another type of skill is required when taking *edges*.
Slithering away, yet not touching anyone the rider pledges.
Hit someone, and you could be thrown into the hedges.
Skill and mastery the rider displays, otherwise he alleges.

Riding fast or riding slow, be careful how you go.

Riding up and down, racing on Great George's Street.
Cycling friends you pass, you'd always greet.
Navigating trucks and cars seemed so sleek.
Riding daily to school five days a week.

Riding fast or riding slow, be careful how you go.
Living in Westmoreland, your riding skill you advance,
Should not be seen as random or just perchance.
As young and old female and male,
Riding always to tell their tale.

Riding fast or riding slow, be careful how you go.

So many children rode to school,

Navigating public spaces and looking cool.

Riding one hand or freehand,

Getting attention and feeling grand.

For adults their means of transportation,

Riding many miles was no exaggeration.

Riding fast or riding slow, be careful how you go.

Bicycle riding is for all.

Look at my bruises, evidence from the fall.

Learn the skill that's the call.

For work or for fun,

Just riding in the sun.

Fearful ones will have none.

Riding for me, as a child I begun.

Riding fast or riding slow, be careful how you go.

23 - Gigs We Play

Lunchtime, breaktime, or evening time after school,
Who's playing gigs and whose will dominate?
Big, medium, or small it doesn't matter the size,
Playing gigs causes excitement, all will accommodate.
Multicoloured gigs in motion, the colours illuminate.

Gigs we made from different wood.
Guava, soursop, or cedar wood.
Heavy and sturdy the rigours it withstood.
A throw of the gig and spinning as it should.
The point deliberately smooth and firm,
To split a gig, you'd see the owner squirm.

Dominating the ring, making you feel good.

Little boys playing gigs, the excitement of childhood.

But look, the gigs are spinning beyond a minute,

Even with time there appears to be no limit.

Spinning and spinning in one place,

All in the contest, which one will last the longest?

First to end is last, but to the very end you've won the contest.

Then and only then your gig is the best.

That zinging sound the gigs make.

Revolutions per second is the rate.

Spinning and spinning, the competition is at stake.

Excitement peaked, it won't abate.

Everyone so intense as we all partake.

Smooth and motionless the gigs appear.

All spinning so fast in full gear.

Little boys are excited, at the gigs they stare.

Time for home, did you boys hear?

The Principal's instruction as reaching late was her fear.

Just a quick *scorn di eart* before we go,

This the boys thought was the real show.

Catching the gig before it reaches the ground.

Skillfully, the boys have the gig spinning in their palm.

Intently looking and appearing calm,
What prowess you'd say, experts in form.

Playing gigs as boys, even spinning on the forearm.
Chatty friends, with your skills you'd disarm.
None can test you; your gig and skill are the best.
All the arguments they had, you put to rest.
Fun time with gigs and winning the contest.
Nothing more exciting, the thrill, now the conquest.
It's time for home and Mum with her inquest.

24 - Marbles We Play

Playing marbles requires concentration and skill.
Knuckle down and shoot the marble, oh what a thrill.
Hitting the opponent's marble out of the ring.
Such marksman-like aim you take, the objective to fulfil,
As daily we practised our marble skill.

Use your opportunity wisely from the very beginning,
As you compete with the intention of winning.
Missing the target in the ring, you might be regretting,
As your opponent gets a chance which may be upsetting.

But as we play, we persevere to the end.

Such simple instructions we will commend.

As an opportunity so quickly may arise,

For this you must prepare, there should be no surprise.

Daily we played marbles just for fun.

Under the cool shade of the trees or in the blazing sun.

Losing the game, yourself only to blame,

Winning requires diligence and practice, it's that plain.

It is your choice, our game, is success your aim?

25 - Common Entrance Exam Results

Just a normal Saturday afternoon when the family would commune.

The evening's music we attuned, as all gathered in the dining room.

Son, go fetch a serving spoon.

Soon the evening's meal was over, siesta time, now going to my room.

In the car Mum and Dad went, like a mission they were sent.

60 minutes later, down the hill they sped.

Heading back home as if on a sleigh they sled.

Dad while driving, the cheering he led.

Mum looked gleeful and happy, not a word she said.

Holding *The Gleaner*, for information he read.

Seated on the veranda without knowing what to think.

In the chair I curled, feeling like a shrink.

Why so much excitement? I couldn't make the link.

His happy persona one would think,
Dad's bright smile and a wink.
Permit me one, a celebratory drink.
Common Entrance Exams you successfully inked.
Come look in *The Gleaner*, your unique name is in print.
For the college of your choice, now you can rejoice.

What a feeling it was, both happy and sad.
Going to Munro College, for this I was glad.
This was increased costs, for both Mum and Dad.
Another high school expense, for them now to add.
The family income is limited and small, how could parents manage it all?

Simple khaki pants and shirt we all must wear,
Standard boy's uniform representing the basic gear,
With shiny black shoes, requiring only a pair.
No matter what, this was a dream come true,
Boys of similar calling, now a part of the crew,
Wearing and supporting the gold and blue.

Mum quickly left the car,
A hug and a kiss for her son.
It's time to have some fun.
You did it, but you're not yet done.

This is just the beginning, more successes to come.

Continue to pray my son, work hard, you'll overcome.

Three siblings now attending high school,

All were told, education is the tool,

For advancement, it's simply the rule,

All the other children wanted it too.

Two more siblings to follow,

Work hard and do not sorrow.

Mum's beating, we abhor,

Working hard it implores.

What a celebratory time it was,

Family members happy and abuzz.

All basking in my success,

To God I must confess,

As He allowed my progress.

But other students were also glad,

Success they attained, new heights to be gained.

Their school of choice, some obtained.

Yet others cried, were momentarily untamed,

As the score required, they did not attain.

Another year to wait to change their state.

As the Common Entrance Examination determines your fate.

26 - The Winding Roads

Summer holiday is coming, for children that's exciting,
Principal's plan for the children sounded enticing.
Needing her teachers' agreement before informing,
The children of her intention of a school outing.

Going to Montego Bay would be a special day.
Jamaica's second city a parish away.
The journey by bus was two hours one-way.
On the winding roads, that bus will surely sway.

When the children heard, they started to laugh.
So excited, some started to cough.
Seeking her Dad's permission who generally denies,
Her charm, calm, and coercing skills she now applies.
The Principal said it would be educational,
With a wink and a smile and shedding a tear.

Get your things together my girl, her plans in full gear,
Thanks Dad, as this is a trip oh-so rare.

What's the attire, a question so clear,
Your school uniform you all shall wear.
In your uniform each can be easily identified.
Such a response, all children were satisfied.

Outing to Montego Bay, the Principal started to plan.
Get your confirmation from your parents as early as you can.
One by one the confirmations came in.
Counting the numbers of how many will be coming.

Soon the numbers the Principal could tally,
Requiring a big Champion bus for all to carry.
The morning for the trip so quickly it comes.
Equally excited were Dads and Mums.
Lining up of the children of significant length,
Roll call concluded, on the big bus they went.

From Clapham through to Brighton, on its descent.
Through the winding and rocky road, the big bus went.
Happy children looking through the windows,
Yet the sleepy ones quickly rested on the pillows.

Onto the main road the big bus goes.

Being careful and vigilant, the driver shows,

So frequently the horn he blows,

In a rhythmic manner it all flows.

Navigating the winding roads while changing gears,

A nod of confidence in his skills, relieving our fears.

Hours pass, and soon the scene changes,

Flat sugarcane land, having left behind mountain ranges.

So many concrete buildings, all so close.

Stoplights at road junctions, to manage traffic flows.

A line-up of vehicles now starting to move really slow.

Irritable drivers, their horns they blow,

Demanding movement as frustration grows.

15 minutes later, the bus stops.

Finally, at the airport, we have arrived.

The long winding roads we have survived.

Children, listen carefully please,

Getting lost can happen with so little ease.

All in groups of five, holding each other's hand,

All intently looking as they stand.

Up the stairs onto the waving gallery, they went.

Confused children saw people waving and crying,

Understanding the emotions, the children were trying,
Loved ones leaving, bonds broken, the hurt they're feeling.

But look, what huge aeroplanes people are boarding,
Such a large wingspan with two engines on each wing.
The sucking sound the engines are making,
As final checks the technicians are pursuing.

For minutes, the plane is taxiing.
Now it turns and the speed advances.
The sound of power and the force it expends,
As the plane propels upward and transcends.
Amazing! the little boy said, his presence he defends.
Being a pilot someday, he intends.

Leaving the airport, on to the Rose Hall Plantation,
Meeting the tour guides we extend a salutation.
They call her Annie Palmer, the White Witch, but she is dead.
Don't go looking for her, she's now only a story in your head.
Thank you, Principal, that information is very critical.
As the story of Annie Palmer got me cynical.

What rolling greens and picturesque scenery.
Cut stone walls and wooden floor with sheen.
Utensils seen, worn and dated,

Used by Annie Palmer, so they stated.

What a gruesome story of slavery we're told,

Walking through the house, you must be bold.

Next, to the little zoo we all went,

Trickster monkeys climbing with such intent.

Exotic birds singing with an accent.

Excited children enjoying each moment spent.

Oh what a wonderful day the children had.

School outing was a success, and all were glad.

Annie Palmer caused a little fright,

But slavery was brought to light.

Their fertile minds enlightened,

Their appreciation for school further heightened.

Going home to start holidays in a reflective mood,

Was the Principal's plan as the trip did conclude.

Boarding School Days at
Munro College

"In Arce Sitam Quis Occultabit"
A City Set Upon a Hill cannot be Hid

27 – A City on a Hill

Driving on the narrow roads up onto Santa Cruz Mountain,
Obscuring our vision was the thick fog like a hazy curtain.
Carefully going through, navigating the winding roads,
Likewise, the farmer, on the donkey as he rode.
City on a hill is now our school and abode.

At long last, on the top of the mountain we stood.
Little boy, adopting a new life and brand.
A dream he had, what a college so grand.
Son you're here, this is what we planned.
"Let's walk across."
"Mum, please don't hold my hand."

Up the 17 stairs to the Principal's Office.
With parents in front, the little boy looked like a novice.

Everyone so quiet, seemingly standing in reverence.

Handing over documents for which they reference.

Quietly Dad spoke, his profile of deference.

"Welcome to Munro College young man."

What a serious stare, no smile, did he care?

That stern voice, the young man full of fear.

"The bells you'll hear, you must adhere,

Be on time and always prepare."

Were those words of wisdom he just shared?

With a nod and a smile, the young man was so scared.

Choked up and confused he looked and stared.

Go to your House Master across the terrace,

Coke Farquharson House appears with medieval magnificence.

Another pale-faced man, is he really Jamaican?

House Master, as he spoke, a British man.

Very little courtesy he spared or spent,

Up the thick wooden stairs, we were sent.

Through the dark wooden passage, we went.

Here you are in your dormitory.

Boys chatting and corroboratory.

Bunk beds from which to choose,

Benefits from either, I suppose.

Who cares or who knows,

Just choose a bed, this is how it goes.

Older boys gathered seemingly like a clan,

Laughing and talking under the Arches they stand.

This is your time son, work hard and remember your plan.

Munro College, city on a hill.

The gusty evening air and its chill.

28 - City on a Hill Where We Stood

City on a hill where we stood,

Beside the staff room made from cut stone and wood.

What a lovely view of the fields,

The expanse of the hillside and plains it reveals.

Such beauty you see, you couldn't conceal.

The majestic art, the beauty of nature you feel, yes so real.

City on a hill where we stood, given to the poor and that's so good.

A place of excellence as it should,

Attended by boys from near and far,

Some are so brilliant, on the wall here their names are.

Yet others in their own right became a star.

City on a hill where we stood, just walk around, and see the difference.

Indeed, my choice and preference.

Cut stone walls you must reference.

The history it tells, of great importance,

Within these walls, what a secured feel and assurance.

City on a hill where we stood,

So frequently you'd hear the choir singing.

Near and far, the notes were ringing.

In the chapel were the boys,

Look and listen, every tree had a voice.

The whistling weeping willows you'd hear,

Bent as they sway, and with flair.

City on a hill where we stood,

The chilly mornings of the Christmas term,

See the little boys as they squirm.

So quickly they lined up under the Arches,

One by one they enter as they march in.

Breakfast time, so important,

Older boys are bullying and so discordant.

City on a hill where we stood.

The greens of the trees and fields,

The flowers in the garden and the beauty it yields.

The years we had, and friendships built,

Remain strong and will not wilt.

29 - Run a Boat at City on a Hill

Call it bravery or just foolish,

At the end of the boat, it was always moreish.

Corn beef, ketchup, and five pounds of flour,

Were the ingredients awaiting the hour.

If you're caught, you'll surely cower,

Suspension awaits, that would be so sour.

But oh the thrill to run a boat stands tall like the bell tower.

30 minutes past midnight,

Peace and quiet was just right.

Your group of three all in your sight,

Quietly from the bed, all are upright.

Committed to the boat throughout the night.

All moving around quietly and slow,

Assignments all known, now it's time to flow.

Everyone knows the hot plate will glow,

But the intensity of the heat is very low.

The boat will go no faster than a moke;
Everyone now is under a yoke.

20 minutes and the water remains warm,
Not too hot to cause any harm.
Kneading the flour in your palm,
Undertaking the process with confidence and calm.
Eight dumplings to each pound of flour,
Must now be boiled within the hour.

10 minutes more and the water is bubbling.
Steam it expels, now ready for the dumplings.
30 minutes past two and the pot is cooked.
What a stern face he had as he stared and looked.
How many of you are in this boat?
The four of us of which he took note.

Cold sweat awash and notably in grief,
All four frantic and shaking like a leaf,
The Prefect so stern and looking peeved,
One of the four started to heave.
Breaking the rules, you've started to deceive,
To the House Master you'll go for caning to receive.

With a second thought and a quizzical look,

From the pot, eight dumplings the Prefect took.

With ketchup and corn beef placed on top,

Did he ask, or did he steal from our pot?

It didn't matter now; pardon we have got.

But what a vexed and irate feeling it was,

In the beginning was the hype and the buzz.

The barefaced Prefect has now stolen our food,

Eight dumplings he took, causing a bad mood.

Each of us four boys ate six dumplings,

Satisfying our needs, forgetting the rumblings.

Sharing with friends the rest, now having their nightly rest.

So quickly the floor was swept,

Utensils were washed and all were kept.

10 minutes to four, all went to bed and slept.

Rising early in the morning, no signs of the boat.

Hear the Prefect calling, looking to gloat.

Turning to us he asked, when is the next boat?

Such audacity the Prefect had, exploiting us, which was bad.

Not reporting us we were glad, stealing our food, we were mad.

Running another boat?

Call it bravery or foolish, but not for fad.

30 -Tennis at City on a Hill

Look at the three impressive tennis courts,
In the middle of the campus all would sport.
Proficient players on 'A' court they played,
'C' court for beginners, that's where they stayed.

So many times, we played on 'C' Court,
Learning to coordinate and hit the ball straight.
Little Powa with his coordinates awry,
Hitting the ball away, no matter how he tried.

Into Mrs Roper's garden the ball went,
Searching carefully, as the flowers we bent.
Locating the ball, we patiently searched,
Now back on the court, a more careful stroke emerged.

Teachers' evening for playing the game.

The strokes they made seemed so tame.

Control and accuracy, no other aim.

Cautiously playing to preserve their name.

Intermittent power stroke, creating fame.

But as she walked on the court,

The campus, she had their full support.

Each stroke she made was the requisite,

The pose she made was so exquisite.

Tennis we played just for fun,

Even on Saturdays in the sun.

Mastering the game was the aim,

Getting better each day was our claim.

Powa, he tried but no advances to gain.

'C' court he stayed, despite his passion and flame.

31 - Friendships from City on a Hill

What a big campus it was,
The first day at school with such a buzz.
Little boys and their parents seemingly fearful,
Little boy now left alone feeling tearful.

White man bearded and looking so stern,
Each morning my insides would always churn.
Why was the Class Master talking so firm?
His care for us you could only discern.

But the history of the school we would later learn.
This is your time, make full use of the opportunity.
As old boys are generally respected in their community.
So influential, the old boys now in national leadership.
Munro College, an excellent school, deemed the flagship.

But what fun, being part of a close-knit community,

Living with so many boys mostly in unity.

The bullying and teasing, yes you suffer,

Made you stronger and even tougher.

Boys you saw throughout the days,

Learning their style and their ways.

Allowing you to identify those who care,

Perhaps one day with them, your *tuck* you'd share.

As the days went by, bonds of friendship became so deep.

Even beyond school, the bonds we keep.

As boys become men,

A phone call every now and then.

The friendships, so deep, are what you reap.

32 - Hop Time at City on a Hill

What excitement throughout senior school,
Boys well dressed and appearing to be cool.
The afro we wore neatly groomed,
Hop at Hampton, girls thoroughly perfumed.

Disembarking the bus with groove and style,
Looking all around wearing a pleasant smile.
Wow, look at his *bell foot* pants with such flair,
His brightly coloured floral shirt and his curly hair.
As he entered the hall, he could feel the stare.

Looking around, so many lovely young ladies,
All well put together and blooming like daisies.
Having a chat with two and the heart it eases.
My accolades they appreciated and that pleases.
Now it's time to ask for a dance if it so appeases.

But so many boys just leaning against the wall.

A smile and an outstretched hand that was all.

Nothing more you needed to do; she understood the call.

A fear of rejection, they said, would cause them to feel small.

But not asking the ladies, they felt hurt and appalled.

Wondering why young men came to the party at all.

But listen, it's the final ballad to be played,

Suddenly before you she swayed.

Instead of you asking, she did,

The dance we had and goodbye she bids.

33 - Peg Leg at City on a Hill

A wooden foot he had, pulling it on the board floor,
Was there some truth or a Munro lore?
The loud sounds clearly heard within the dorms.
The sound coming closer, wondering if he'll harm,
Frantic boys in bed, all trying to keep calm.

A wooden foot he had, pulling it on the board floor,
With a step and pull, sounding even louder.
What an eerie feeling, so frightening,
Our peaceful spirit it was disturbing.
For clueless boys it was very disconcerting.
As we sat up in our beds, some started praying.

A wooden foot he had, pulling it on the board floor,
Did I hear someone clearing their throat?
Indeed! There's someone in a long dark coat.

Swiftly he disappeared, causing me to feel so afraid.

Where did this come from, he must have strayed.

A wooden foot he had, pulling it on the board floor,

Was it my imagination just taunting me?

Looking down the passage again, yes it is he.

The tall striking image of our Prefect, I now see.

It wasn't Peg Leg, as he watched and had a spree.

Be quiet, he frantically beckoned, was his plea.

A wooden foot he had, pulling it on the board floor,

It wasn't a wooden foot this time, but a hockey stick.

Pulling it on the board floor, what imagery, creating an uproar.

Please mister Prefect, no more jokes, as Peg Leg stories we abhor.

Boys were upset and angry, some even swore.

Back to bed we went, some started to snore.

34 - Bobo Ski Watten Talla Alla Ski Wah

Football season and the school in a frenzy.

Winning the DaCosta Cup, was it imaginary?

Brazilian coach with a lovely personality,

The passion for the game, boys training regularly.

Opponents driving up Santa Cruz Mountain each year,

Just the history of Munro College caused them great fear.

That carpeted green field, they stood and stared,

The air so cool, seemingly so rare.

Listen to the cheer as to the heavens it soars.

Boys with their thunderous voices as they roar.

Listen all around, the cheer reverberates.

How much more can our opponents tolerate?

But those were the days when the team was classy.

Fit boys using the Brazilian style of short passes.

Moving the ball around, starting from the back,

With such poise and control, what a wonderful attack.

Early in the tournament, the games we would win.

Passing the ball so smoothly, opponents in a spin.

But as the tournament advances, the cheer ceases,

More difficult were the games, our style in pieces.

Winning the DaCosta Cup, was it really imaginary?

Support for our team, they got unconditionally.

What fun we had with those thunderous shouts.

The opponents, we thought, would buckle and doubt.

Summer and Christmas Holidays

The excitement that ensued during our favourite times of the year.

35 - Christmas Eve in Town

Poinsettia red and Jasmine white herald the season bright.

Cooler evenings support your rest throughout the night.

Shorter days and longer nights make the spirit light.

Time of year where there's fun, to everyone's delight.

Christmas time again,

Christmas time for all.

Are you hearing the call?

Children on holiday are so excited,

Revising scripture verses to be recited,

The story of His birth reignited,

At church, Christmas morning, all are invited.

Christmas time again,
Christmas time for all.
Are you hearing the call?

But on the Eve, there is so much excitement.
Great George's Street is brightly lit as part of the complement.
Purposeful people reflecting the season's enticement,
Purchasing gifts and tokens, expressing their sentiment.

Christmas time again,
Christmas time for all.
Are you hearing the call?

Beside the courthouse, the tall and brightly lit Christmas tree.
Lights of different colours for all to see.
Children gathered in their multicoloured hats, full of glee.
Blowing their horns on Christmas Eve, it's like a jamboree!

Christmas time again,
Christmas time for all.
Are you hearing the call?

But the beating of the bass drum gets louder,
The heightened pitch of the flute gets clearer.

The large crowd moved to the rhythm of the beat.

Congestion all across Great George's Street.

It's horse head, the pregnant lady et al, all on parade.

Rocking to the beat, look it's masquerade!

Christmas time again,

Christmas time for all.

Are you hearing the call?

Little children screaming and in a frenzy.

Terror and fear on their little faces showed aplenty.

Masquerade is coming closer and closer.

Oh how it appears as if they are teasing.

Little children hiding, the sight is less than pleasing.

Christmas time again,

Christmas time for all.

Are you hearing the call?

Within minutes the beat fades, walking to the stores now accelerates.

But look at the star lights bright and sparkling, clappers exploding and crackling.

Christmas Eve activities pitched and sizzling.

Christmas time again,

Christmas time for all.

Are you hearing the call?

What a time of excitement in the heart of the town, tired legs
our minds bemoan.

Friends we greeted; now no longer can we roam.

It's Christmas Eve and time for home,

Presents bought, now to tally the sum;

Mum's sorrel and pudding, I'll have some.

Christmas time again,

Christmas time for all.

Are you hearing the call?

36 – Palate to Tease

Christmas conjures a lot of excitement.
Even sometimes a lot of merriment.
It's family time and coming together,
Mother, father, sons and daughters.

Christmas conjures a lot of excitement.
Food, drink, and cake for enticement.
Moderation displaced as restraint has no hold.
Importantly, I can't ignore the aspect of our soul.

Christmas conjures a lot of excitement.
Rum-laced sorrel and wine from a barrel.
Pig now converted to bacon and ham,
Let's not forget the chicken and the lamb.

Christmas conjures a lot of excitement.

Gungo rice and peas if you please,

It's all good for the palate to tease.

Body mass index expands with ease.

Christmas conjures a lot of excitement.

He was born, but some had resentment,

Virgin birth did not create contentment.

His origin defied the establishment.

Christmas conjures a lot of excitement.

Thanking God for His Son's birth,

In Bethlehem right here on earth.

Now let's understand His invaluable worth.

Christmas conjures a lot of excitement.

The research is done, and history has won,

Jesus Son of God has come.

Help me Lord amidst the fun,

To acknowledge Him and serve the Son.

37 – Independence

In 1962, there was one of two,
To one we became true.
Size wasn't a clue, small, medium, or huge.
It didn't matter your hue; nation building was the glue.

Lowering the Union Jack, now being sent back.
British oversight sacked,
Jamaica's leadership on track to watch the nation's back.

Gold, green and black.
Hoisting the National Flag, for which most people were glad.
What hype and excitement, even for a moment.
People consider the future, it's just around the corner.

Pomp and pageantry on display, many colours in array.
Bustamante or Manley, wages remained paltry.

Shackles of yesteryear, no longer shall we wear.
For Independence time is here, preparation in full gear.

School children revising, poems they are reciting,
Festival competition arriving, their skills they must believe in,
The prize that they can win.

Teachers patiently prepared,
Students postured and compared.
For words they properly pronounced,
Breathing paused, voices bounced.
Participating in festival brings clout.

Here the adults come, the competition, they wanted some.
Singing of culture and life, competing for festival song.
Soon the winner is announced, containment is renounced
As the crowd sang and danced, to their favourite song they
pranced.

Look here comes masquerade!
Drumming, dancing all on parade.
Little children so easily scared,
Mum and Dad to their aid.

What a climax so bright, Independence giving sight.
For festival we delight, to make the people light.
Independence and festival time, together they came as one.
So much time has gone, has the nation really won?
Progression or regression, look to our history,
What a period so thorny, a nation with a story.

38 – Camp Time

So many apprehensions around camp.
Why would parents be so reluctant?
Grandparents likewise are resistant,
Yet, for my sister Pet, it was sheer excitement.

A closing position my parents delayed,
After rants and arguments my sister made.
Finally, our parents claimed they were swayed,
By arguments from my sister's lengthy crusade.
To camp you can go, but sounding enraged.

Suitcase packed and off my sister went.
To Moorlands Camp on roads narrow and bent.
Remember the money that's being spent.
Such a position, who wouldn't resent?
Report to the leaders any forms of discontent.

Remember your well-being is our intent.
Your safety we must ensure to the fullest extent.

Like-minded parents concerned and weary,
Pondering their decision, made it scary.
Their teenage children, for them they are fearing.
Look at the other children, all seem to vary,
Tall and strong, some seemed daring.
Some chatty, others quiet but most seemed caring,
Some good signs, for the parents, are partially assuring.

A week at camp, she experienced growth,
Verses she read, she started to quote.
A wonderful experience, how she has grown.
Positive thoughts, so many were sown.
No longer should our parents frown.

Seeing the experience she had,
In my mind, for me it was a nod.
Going to camp next year, surely, I'll be glad.

Saving camp fees, I started then.
Showing parents, going to camp, I'm bent.
No need to worry, my sister went.
I'm sure my experience will be equivalent.

Another year has passed,

Summertime again, camp for me at last.

What a twisted face she cast,

Your Dad you must ask.

Mum, from last year we spoke,

My feelings you now evoke.

Dad, you know, is not here.

Tonight, when he comes, he won't hear.

How do I know he will even care?

Anyhow, for camp I will prepare.

Please Mum, my mother dear.

Early in the morning Dad shouted,

No camp for you, you are grounded.

The reason for the decision was not stated,

My hope and desire wasn't deflated.

Your best position is to visit your grandparents,

As your mother and sisters make holiday arrangements.

Never mind my Dad, I'll stay with you.

He had not a thought, idea, or clue,

That my trip to camp I've revamped.

No longer did I need Dad to transport me there.

As I saved up adequate funds for the bus fare.

Throughout the day I drove around with Dad.

We made various stops including by a shop.

In the distance I saw a car coming.

Quickly I alighted from ours and started thumbing.

Company for the driver, he quickly said come in.

Grabbing my iron box of clothes from inside our car,

While waving goodbye as Dad stood afar.

On my way to Teen Time Camp.

My desire no longer they will cramp.

Dad said, that little scamp.

So lovely were the days.

Reading the Bible and singing praise.

Without understanding my parents' apprehensions,

Camp for me supported my convictions.

Did parents care about the friends I met?

The days went by with no incident of regret.

The leaders and campers were friendly,

Three meals a day were always plenty.

Chilly nights there required a blanket,

On the very last day what a lovely banquet.

39 – Summer Time

It's summer term now school has ended.

School results made me sad.

No longer my worry, for holiday I am glad.

Boarding school we went, the making of ladies and gents.

Now it's time for home, with space to walk and roam.

Seeing Mum smiling, the first sign of home.

Birds, dogs, and cats, with all we had a chat.

As we walked and greeted, new offspring to meet.

Pets so quickly walked to us, seemingly to a beat.

Just a week at home, with both Mum and Dad,

Now being sent to grandparents for which we were glad.

To the town of Grange Hill, we cycled and walked at will.

This is a sugarcane town, where sugar is made brown.

Grandpa was a farmer, daily the provisions he'd garner.

So diligently he worked, feeding the family got harder.

Sumptuous meals we had on a budget oh-so meagre.

Grandma's skills displayed, mastery she portrayed.

Meals consumed without delay, for each we had to pray.

Early to rise, a word that's wise.

Delaying our rise was the neighbour's prize,

As juicy orange mangoes became their morning's heist.

Our mangoes we were denied, our home they defiled.

Tomorrow's another day, our rise we won't delay.

What a lovely smell it gives, the majority of life it lives.

The aroma it sends, taunting your senses,

Morning, noon, and night.

This is when you know jackfruit is full and ripe.

Picking the fruit by climbing the tree,

Eating the fruit, the smile and glee.

Lunchtime was porridge time,

An experience so sublime.

Homemade cornmeal, or banana time.

No one waited on the clock to chime.

Whatever the type, there was a hype.

The bowl clean, we'd wipe.

With two pear trees in the yard, the battered fruits you discard.

A pear or two was there to share, big or small, we didn't care.

Bread and pear, bulla and pear, whichever way you liked it.

With every meal or snack, it was always a delightful fit.

Lemonade we so frequently made,

Lemonade with a dark brown shade,

Homemade lemonade was of good grade.

Dinner with lemonade, you just wouldn't trade.

As evening sets, pots are placed under cover.

A bath you have, instead of a shower,

With sun heated water outside for over an hour.

Read a book grandson, a boring request or desire.

The appetite for such, I'm yet to acquire.

Soon the holiday comes to an end, now it's back to school again.

New uniforms Mum bemoans, as the children all have grown.

To Seven Stars Store Mum goes, no longer in a groan.

Children's uniforms acquired, now outfitted as required.

Something More

The variety, style and colour of country living etched in our hearts.

40 - Big Dutch Pot

Light brown pudding with gravy on top.
Serving starts now, look everything stops.
Deep long cut in the big dutch pot.
Here comes your slice with gravy on top.

Cornmeal pudding or potato pudding,
It doesn't matter which type you're baking.
As long as there's pudding for the taking,
Here we come, pudding we are eating.

Coal pot set and the fire starts to catch,
The fire on top of equal match.
In between is the big dutch pot,
With a lovely mixture and spices on top.

Sugar and flavours as part of the mixture,

Coconut milk aids with the texture.

Vanilla and cinnamon whip up the taste,

Fifty minutes of baking finished, no haste.

Everybody hearing pudding is baking.

One takes the coconut and quickly starts grating.

Leaves on the ground, someone starts raking.

Everyone responsive, pudding we're awaiting.

Work and pudding are a special match,

Just say the word and all will attach.

Chores assigned, all done with dispatch.

Floor is cleaned, leaving not a scratch.

Work may be hard, but with pudding all is in your catch.

41 - Mango Time

All throughout the community there were mango trees.

Big, medium, and small mango trees you will all see.

Brown trunks and branches with leaves all green.

Laden mango trees, what an appealing and lovely scene.

Some fruits have a tinge of red but mostly green.

Others are fully green and some have a sheen.

Everyone watching all looked keen, each fruit inspected; each speck seen.

Who will pick it, inspectors beyond sixteen?

Everyday all are watching until bright yellow is seen.

Trees near the road are viewed more than the rest.

Ownership, they say, is of little or no interest.

Passers-by all, watching so keenly and intense.

Waiting patiently to pick the fruit without breaching the fence.

High in the tree, three mangoes are bright yellow,
The fruits are matured and now are looking mellow.
On the roadside, a lovely view from below,
Taste buds activated, here comes the flow.
Picking those mangoes, needing to be a pro.

Sinking your teeth in and peeling back the skin.
What a big bite, the flesh so juicy within.
Feeling the juice, now running down your chin.
Eating those mangoes, a bellyful within.
Can't wait any longer, now I'm in a spin.

Climbing the tree, for those three I see,
In itself is a challenge, one must flee.
The tree so huge, climbing isn't for me.
So tall is this tree, a slight breeze would set them free.
Or toppled to the ground, you could be sent,
If the limb breaks when it is bent.

Pray O God, do send breeze to make the limb sway,
That somehow as it sways, the fruits will drop our way.
Midday gone, now the whole day,
Not a breeze to help or just to sway.

Next morning the three mangoes disappeared.
So disappointed I was, now full of despair.

In a quest to understand the mystery on the ground,

With one throw of the stone, many tumbled down.

A passer-by, they said, picked more than the three.

In a few short moments the mangoes were his own.

Mangoes you must watch until fully grown,

You can't call them yours even when the tree you own.

Eyes all around, keenly watching all of them,

Carefully to note, yet no one you can condemn.

As pickers all seem to be invisible men.

It didn't matter what type of mango,

Hairy, Stringy, or Common Mango,

Bees Box, Graham, or Scissors Mango.

Number Eleven, Robin, Green Gauge Mango.

Once the name is mango, you must pick them to call them your own.

Patience you must display, until fully grown.

42 – Crop Time

What a busy period it becomes when it's crop time.

Look as far as you can, on the flatlands called George's Plain.

Tall, slender and grass-like plant known as sugarcane,

Matures in 12 months, from which sugar we gain.

Harvested in season with minimal rain.

Maximum returns are our farmers' aim.

Men in their hundreds start at the dawning of the day,

To cut cane by the measure, tirelessly earning their way.

Cutting square after square without any delay.

Fortnightly they gather to get their meagre pay.

With an early start, they benefit from the cool morning.

As the tropical sun can be very scorching.

But look, all long-sleeved shirts they are wearing.

As the long-leaved blades cause severe itching.

Look beyond, sugarcane fields are burning.

Ridding fields of rodents and insects which may be lurking.

Floating soot, playful children tried catching.

Billowing smoke, thick and dark,

The crackling of the fire as it drifts and sparks.

Freshly washed linen, now discoloured as the ash marks.

Disgruntled housewife, another labour of love, she harks.

Is there anyone to listen to our plight she asks?

Washing her linen again, a duplicated task.

Piles of cut sugarcane now on the ground,

Ready for collection, sugarcane all around.

Tractors with laden carts, to the factory they're bound,

To process dark brown sugar crystals, in homes to be found.

But for the small farmer, his sugarcane to garner.

Donkey-drawn drays, pulling cane away.

Tomorrow is another day, as the beasts of burden sway.

Hardworking donkey, up and down it goes,

But in the evenings, it's time to repose.

Miles away the factory's tall white exhausts are seen.

Thick, dark billows of smoke as housewives watch keen.

All an indication of the factory, oh what a busy scene,

In support of fortnightly pay, despite being paltry and lean.

Adjoining towns are full of hype.

Trading extended of different types.

Sugarcane industry expanded commerce,

Creating opportunities, none were averse.

As early in the mornings some cane cutters converse.

Should I put my pay in my wife's purse?

43 - Culloden by the Sea

Little district on the southern coast of Westmoreland.
Undulating in form and bordered by the Caribbean Sea.
Each morning you arise, the deep blue you'd see.
Quiet country district with ordinary folk, all would agree.

But what a picturesque scene is painted.
The gentle sloping hillside, with thousands of coconut trees.
The branches and leaves flowing, in the gentle breeze.
Brown boughs with yellow branches and leaves,
All following in the direction as the wind leads.
On the hillside with a gentle sloping grade,
Coconut trees bearing nuts and providing shade.

What about the dark brown, Jamaica Red cows?
Grazing on the lands with their heads they bow.
As they walk, they rub on the bough.
Free ranged and looking full and firm,
Majestic Jamaican cow.

In their midst you would not permit your friend or foe,
As a strange person there, they would not allow.

Swimming in the peaceful sea in the calm of the morning,
Looking out, a small fisherman's boat slowly sailing through,
It's just a speck on the deep and light blue hue.
What an expanse of blue, where it ends, where is the clue?
There goes a seagull, effortlessly it flew.
In search of breakfast, it dawdles through.
So urgently needed for strength to accrue.

The busyness of the day creeps up on all.
Ordinary people like farmers, shopkeepers,
Vendors, teachers, housewives, clerks must answer the call.
Hastily walking the street are people short and tall.
Up and down they go in the direction of their call.

Here is the New Hope Primary School.
Education for growth is the children's tool.
On the seaside it is perched.
In its midst there is the quaint Moravian Church.
Happy children up and about all eager to learn.
Day by day and early in the mornings they return.
What aptitude they displayed, so focused and intense.
As their ambitions for high school, they quickly reference.

But on the greens of this church school grounds,

Is history that is laid bare.

Headstones of locals and foreigners, at us they stare

Valuable information if at all we care.

Blacks and whites alike, the same grounds they share.

The closeness they share, they're unaware.

But what does it even matter now?

On that morn, to Him all will bow.

Here come the boys all dressed in khaki pants and shirts.

For the teenagers, their epaulettes differentiate,

The high school of progress or their fate.

As the bus for school, they await.

Here come the high school girls in their pleated blue uniforms,

Starched and ironed, to the school rules they conform.

White and blue or checkered blue tops, their association, they inform.

Well put together uniforms, what a way they transform.

But what a distracting sound it was,

As the waves broke and dashed against the rocks.

Every piece of clothing removed including their socks.

As boys took their swim round about 3 o'clock.

Swimming during school time, there was a block.

As the strict Principal policed and took stock.

Distraction you must block, education you just don't mock.

But across the road from the school was the village bar.

Its opening hours were restricted and carefully observed.

Evening time, wherever they were, there the men are.

Laughter and chats over drinks with friends as they spar.

Loudly, the jukebox played for all to hear, even from afar.

Sharon, my sister, learnt the songs and sang like a star.

But when the time comes, crocus bags and bottle torches.

To the wetlands and morass, so diligent were the searches,

For crabs in abundance of different sizes.

A shifty crab, so carefully you must hold.

Catching it is for the brave and the bold.

Clamping your finger, your cries the heavens behold.

After school, Owen and I met by the fence.

After a short conversation, playing marbles made sense.

Young boys not bothered with schoolwork so intense,

Would rather have light moments and play with friends.

So many Friday evenings, cashew nuts we roasted.

Our expertise we generally promoted.

Cashews atop the fire caused such a blaze.

The oil it released created such a glaze.

So much smoke it generated, creating a haze.

The many nuts we roasted, so quickly they disappeared.

Our sisters had them all, the assistance they volunteered.

This little seaside district was for all.

It didn't matter your status or call.

Children and adults, even a vendor from a stall.

People big and small.

Culloden by the sea, oh that tall and bulky cotton tree!

The expanse of its branches and shade it advances.

Culloden by the sea, our favourite district for all to see.

44 - Flying High or Low

Birds flying high or low, birds all over.
In the tree for a berry or just for cover.
Birds and their plumage of different colour.
Big or small, on the move, minutely in the hour.
Mornings through to evenings, birds all over.

But the small busy and brown Ground Dove,
Quickly picking away while on the move.
Little boy with a bird's eye view from above,
Ground Dove found on the ground in the grove.
Fearfully picking away, the small Ground Dove.

What a suspicious fable or tale,
If its demise is your aim.
Ghost stories on your trail,
Such a reward like a grail.

Little boy, be careful you don't get lame.

Ground Dove, don't you catch or maim.

Is it really a singing or a noisy bird?

Flying from tree to tree her singing is heard.

Early in the mornings she blasts her notes.

But as the hawk comes, a crusty note so curt.

Nightingale with notes, you dear not hurt.

Understand her singing which comes on time.

Her peaceful pieces in the mornings are so sublime.

Seeing a foe, she sounds irate.

Yet a beautiful song she sings to her mate.

Nightingale, with her singing, indicating her state.

But aha the Petchary bird,

So small in frame yet big in heart.

A spirited chord it records, when making a feisty dart.

The hawk attacks her nest,

But retreats and flees with zest,

As the Petchary bird defends,

With bravery on her quest.

Fearless Petchary bird, you dear not test.

Gracefully the Baldpate flies.

With a catapult the little boy tries,

The Baldpate to catch but it denies,

Ascending higher in the skies,

With dark blue hue and full feathers,

Rain or shine it weathers.

The cooing sound as it dithers,

A calming song, the boy considers.

A shiny blue coating around its neck,

Berries in the tree it would peck.

Bright white crown on its head.

The palm tree berries it prefers instead.

But the lengthy black-billed Woodpecker,

With its distinctive red crown and multicoloured feathers.

Flying around, chirping merrily on its own.

Its burrowing sound heard far away,

Wondering how many holes it burrows each day?

Birds flying high or low, birds all over.

In the tree for a berry or just for cover.

Birds and their plumage of different colour.

Hopping Dicks, White-winged Doves, or John-to-Whits.

Just seeing them, what a joy they bring,

Better yet as daily they sing.

Indeed, a message they bring.

Just listen, let's join them as they sing.

45 - Fish Time at Border

Fried fish by itself is a delightful meal,
With fried bammy is the real deal.
Going to Westmoreland, then Border you must stop.
Onion and pepper placed on top.

Zinc covered sheds all by the sea,
Come with me and you will see.
The deep curved road is overshadowed by trees.
Lush, green and beautiful my friends all agree.

Fresh sea fish well-seasoned and prepared,
The taste you'll agree cannot be compared.
With unique seasonings they all declared,
The best fried fish, their customers cheered.
Onion and pepper placed on top.

Stopping at Border, what an experience!

No vendor providing any pre-eminence.

So many vendors, you must contend,

Who will you choose and who will attend?

Everyone with a colourful plate of fish,

Selling a tasty meal, that's their wish.

Your patronage you know you'll extend.

Requiring some space so as not to offend.

All in your face, no longer can you pretend.

Close mark of confusion now needs to end.

Quietly she moved away and without a stir,

Come over here Mister Sweet Sir.

Her endearment and her charm,

Luring you with her modest calm.

My fish was just fried and is still warm.

Onion and pepper placed on top.

Look, my wood fire burns and there's the dutch pot.

The fireside with flames is still very hot.

I'll package some, tell me when to stop.

Onion and pepper placed on top.

With the special seasoning all infused,
A plate with a goat fish he couldn't refuse.
The quality of the meal, he too must rate.
Look at the decorations around the plate.
This is the reason why we made the stop.
Onion and pepper placed on top.

Eating the fish he licked his chops,
Eating the pepper he walked and hopped.
Reaching for a bottle of cold soda pop.
Never before a fish so hot,
Onion and pepper placed on top.

So madam, what's the price for your fried fish?
Tell me Mister Sweet Sir, do you want another dish?
Five freshly fried fish she carefully packaged.
Here you are, thank you for your patronage.
Onion and pepper placed on top.

Oh Mister Sweet Sir do you want some bammy?
This is my boyfriend, his name is Sammy.
Sell Mister Sweet Sir two bags of bammy,
Wood fire and smoke making Sammy clammy,
This is our life Mister Sweet Sir,
Fire and sun are like a double whammy.

So madam, how long are you selling fried fish?
Five years since I left high school.
And I have two children and one is coming soon.
Oh Mister Sweet Sir did you just make a hum?
Things just happen, we live in the slum.
Anyhow we are done, thanks again, this is the sum.

What a tasty meal of fish and bammy,
A partnership in trade was she and Sammy,
Border experience enjoyed by many.
A rustic experience of culture like any,
Just the taste of it, you walk and hop,
With onion and pepper placed on top.

46 - Don't You Stop?

Daily the donkey goes,
With its leader so close.
Sometimes with hampers laden,
The donkey, the beast of burden.

But unladen donkey and leader walking through the alley,
At such times the light spirited leader and donkey would tarry.
Have you ever had a donkey ride he asked?
Full of excitement, in the question I basked.

Riding a donkey has never been on my mind,
But the donkey's owner appeared so kind.
Then I asked about the saddle and the stirrups.
There were none, his response was very abrupt.

Passing by was a little boy.
Hey! are you going to ride the donkey, he interrupts.
So inquisitive, he stopped and watched.
His riding skills proficient and unmatched.

The donkey's broad back, firm and bruised,
Evidence of heavy weight carried or possibly abused.
Here's the sack, the crocus bag to put on its back,
To soften the seat, as a saddle we lack.

But mounting the donkey wasn't an easy job,
Feeling scared, my heart started to throb.
Stretch your torso across the donkey's back,
Lift your right leg, roll over and rock.
Just like that, you've mounted without the sack.

Now the donkey starts walking slowly,
Moving on its way, donkey so lowly.
But the donkey's back was very tough.
Each step it made; the pathway seemed rough.

The discomfort felt, I thought I had enough.

Then the owner said, "don't you stop?"
Soon you'll learn to mount with just a hop.
Suddenly, the donkey started kicking and jumping,
Rodeo style, the seat was thumping.
Uncontrollable donkey running aimlessly,
Little boy so frightened and trying courageously,
Painfully flattened on the ground laying shamelessly.

Let's lift him up and take him home.
The donkey was so excited, let it roam.
Give him a glass of sugar and water,
The bad feeling will go away shortly, if not later.
That little boy, surely was a tinker,
Causing the donkey to switch in a flicker.
Riding a donkey bareback takes will.
Managing an agitated donkey requires skill.

47 - Where's Your Best?

In us there is the best and the worst.

Understanding this quandary, the worst don't you nurse.

What's the circumstance when the worst wants to burst,

Or may quietly be pushing through but indeed must be reversed?

So many circumstances that could lead to this burst.

Be quick to recognize it, otherwise you could be immersed,

Into a life of regrets, and a pit of unrelenting lies.

Stamp out your worst, lest your best it belies.

This we must understand, as our best our worst denies.

But oh a lack of the Living Water brings out the worst.

Drinking of the Living Water to reverse your worst.

As you navigate life, be prudent and wise,

Avoid the circumstances which will lead to your demise.

More of the Living Water, to quench my thirst.
Let the best push through, the worst it will reverse.
My fragile state, please Lord, do observe,
As only the best for you as I serve.

Help me Lord, this defenceless base.
So quickly the best becomes a wretched case.
The devil's guile and craft, you've failed the test.
Causing the question, where's your best?

Throughout life there are many tests.
Keep focused and work hard at your best.
Prayers at all times, to God are addressed,
Never believe in your own strength,
A weak link at its very best.

Prepare yourself, you will be pressed.
Understand life's events, in them there are tests.
Serving your best, nothing less.
This is our calling, remember Christ, His test.
For you and me, He gave His best.

48 - New Market Flood

June 12th, 1979, all appeared normal that day.

Adults rising early and on their way to work.

Everyone including the manager and the clerk.

Everyone was responsive, work they did not shirk.

Farmers and artisans using their tools,

Children rising early and sent to their schools.

Children's focus is now drifting,

To games and camps their attention is shifting,

As holiday time is fast approaching.

Anything else, their time you're encroaching,

Parents so annoyed with their children, now displayed reproach.

As they stridently encouraged children to stay the course.

Near and far, persons completing tasks they had undertaken.

Post office, shops, and bars, to the public they were opened.

Friends met and topical issues so readily were spoken.

The imminent weather was not considered a threatening condition

Valley-like location is New Market Town.

Lush green vegetation with little brown.

Encircled by farms, where ground provisions are grown.

Rural by nature, everyone is known.

Love and respect, all is shown.

Tropical depression or the seeding of the clouds, torrential rains with drops so loud.

Never before such a fearful crowd, as the rain poured, darkness the shroud.

The gushes of water flowing on the ground, centrally directing courses as if it is bound.

Hours later, settees floated, house defences breached,

In bedrooms water had reached, rising waters, the heavens unleashed.

Safety and security was the focus; no longer were the grounds porous.

Rising waters ready to choke us, wailing farm animals no longer the focus.

Their screeching sounds are fading around us.

Furniture and appliances no longer important, leaving home
for the rains were constant.

Saving lives was everyone's rant, quickly get out, was
people's chant.

Hours of rain and rising waters, the morning dawning slowly
saunters.

Living arrangements, how it alters, people dislocated and
reasoning falters,

Everything they owned was now gone with the waters.

What a catastrophe on the town, what was land now became
underground.

What was land was nowhere to be found, the night's act, all
minds it confounds.

A vast expanse of water, all around is brown.

Covering houses, post office, shops, and bars,

Inventory, cash, revenue stamps, and cars.

Precious little was left but looking at the stars.

As inward thoughts, internally spar.

Nothing could've prevented this natural cause.

The following days were cries and bawls.

Sympathetic persons helping all around.

Gifts and tokens for which there were calls,

Came rolling in as Jamaicans were appalled.
The destruction within a night's fall,
Causing chaos, bringing the town to a crawl.

Living 10 miles away from the town was considered near,
Was no guarantee the showers you would be spared.
Flooding may not have been in your sphere,
It allowed you, dislocated persons to share.
Showing a heart of compassion and care.

Government agencies all activated,
Nearby schools into homes converted.
Politicians busily consulted,
Appearing compassionate and involved,
To identify and support the affected,
Providing food, clothing, and comfort for all.
The request for housing was a desperate call.

Such sterling support from the US Marines,
With equipment to complement local agencies.
Tirelessly working, extended commitments.
Our Lower House's acknowledgement in Parliament,
Extending recognition for support during our predicament.

Motorboats sailed the dark brown waters,
Identifying the marooned and wounded.
Listing the names as they counted,
For an accurate report to be submitted.

What distress seeing floating remains,
The heart and soul it definitely stains.
No reason at this stage to complain.
The trip made was in vain,
No one anticipated such pain,
Neither the expanse that the water had claimed.

For a couple of years, the evidence remained,
As the months passed, there were shoals.
Children swimming, parents scold.
Jamaicans visiting, taking strolls.
New Market Town, now renowned.

Now the water is fully drawn,
Activities in the town are restored.
The people's resilience is adored.
New Market Town, history has shown.
Went way under, but now has grown.

49 - Schoolboy

Up and down he went on the rocky pathway,
His heavy and burly body as he would sway.
The rhythmic clattering you'd surely hear,
Telling the story, Schoolboy is near.

So gentle he was while you rode,
Navigating the rough while we strode.
So many potholes on the road,
Didn't bother him even with a load.

That spotless brown and shiny colour.

Bit and bridle like a collar,

Aid with instructions he took so stellar.

A horse like him you'd always honour.

Long and flowing was his tail,

Upward was his head without fail,

A stroke on his forehead he always liked.

Down the road we went for a ride.

Schoolboy so calm, what a lovely stride.

But look at him galloping along the way,

So full of energy; moving without delay.

His long and effortless stride they all did say,

Surely made him a winner each and every day.

Watching his majestic prowess, minutely I'd replay.

Everybody loved him and wanted a ride,

Nothing more for them than standing by his side.

What a special horse, Schoolboy, for which we cared,

Our favourite horse we all declared.

50 - Pear Culture

Small, medium or big pear tree,

Wine red or green skin pear.

Watery or dry, oval shape or round.

Together, summer and pear time come around.

Those with trees would always hear,

Do you have any avocado pear?

Look at the green and lovely pear tree.

Each day they keenly watch the tree,

Delicate blossoms all would see.

A well-laden tree all would agree,

Fruits maturing in about 120 days.

Pear tree looks good, your neighbour says.

But what joy it is, just giving a pear,

Or even receiving a dry and round pear.

Pear culture of giving and receiving.

Bulla and pear, people in the community are eating.

It's giving,

It's receiving.

It's caring,

Just sharing.

Everyone mostly eating pear.

What a satisfying feeling as you share,

Such a generous act, showing you do care.

Feeling the love, those far and near.

Pear culture, deep in our hearts, cherished so dear.

Give a pear,

Receive a pear,

Share a pear,

Yes we care.

51 - Outdoor Cooking

Cooking outdoors, what a special thing,
Just the thought of it has an exciting ring.
Such energy it creates, walking with a spring,
White rice, mutton, and condiments you'll be taking.
What hype you feel, the music plays while you sing.
Cooking outdoors is a special thing.

Finally, the wood fire is caught and is burning,
Carefully stoking the fire, the wood you are turning,
To keep it burning with a constant blaze.
That grey smoke it generates causing a haze,
Burning your watery eyes as you gaze.

Wood fire cooking creates such a craze.
Cooking outdoors is a special thing.

As the meal is cooked, the pots are covered in soot.
Just the taste of the meat, what a delightful flavour!
Such mouth-watering taste you'll always want to savour.
Smoked-filled cooking, what a lovely taste,
Under the mango tree, eating without haste.
Thick, yellowish-green curry running like a paste,
Sucking it through the bones, as nothing you waste.
Cooking outside is a special thing.

Curry goat and white rice,
Anytime you'd say, it's always so nice,
Requiring servings at least twice.
Coriander is used as a special spice,
Margarine, you apply for a shelly white rice.
Cooking outside is a special thing.

The word gets around, there's cooking outside.
Many will come, as if in your home they reside.
Some of the servings you discreetly hide.
Some servings you make so very small,
As curry goat and white rice is a favourite of all.
Hungry belly neighbours wanting more.

Cooking outside, what a special thing.

Drinking sweet jelly coconut water to wash it down,

It doesn't matter if the husk is green, yellow, or brown.

Quenching your thirst as the temperature gets hotter.

For many, there's work to be done, but really it doesn't matter,

While eating curry goat and white rice in a box or on a platter.

Creating such fun, hype, laughter, and chatter.

Cooking outside, what a special thing.

52 - Peppered Shrimps

Middle Quarters here we go,

Through mountain ranges and plains.

No rush, just taking it nice and slow,

For the roads in some places are narrow and winding.

Other drivers speed, fast like lightning.

Now we have reached and stopped on the street.

The hype we heard, peppered shrimps we shall eat,

The noisy and assertive vendors likewise to meet.

But here the vendors are,

Briskly approaching and surrounding the car.

Focused and confidently talking, all like a star.

"Good to see you mister, are you coming from afar?"

A little smile and a twang, sounding bizarre.

"Delicious, peppered shrimps we have, here you are."

Locally grown and naturally farmed,

Freshly cooked and packaged.

Madam, is it really an adage?

Is your peppered shrimp the best?

With her bright eyes and full of zest.

Just have a taste, you do the test.

Here's a taste just for you,

Oh! that little shrimp, all red is the hue,

With pepper seeds stuck on as if with glue.

So small is this little shrimp, which alone has the clue.

This little red peppered shrimp spiced appropriately too.

So peppery is the taste,

Sticking to your lips like paste.

Drinking water with such haste.

Peppered shrimps, so quickly, your calm spirit will efface.

First class peppered shrimps; I now rest my case.

Peppered shrimps you asked, Middle Quarters is the place.

53 - Has Time Really Moved On ?

The morning has dawned,
The air is fresh and clean.
The birds are chirping,
The sun is gradually shining.
Has time really moved on?

Each day looks like the day that was.
Sometimes it is overcast and raining.
Indeed, is it really raining?
The throbbing pain of today and yesterday.
Has time really moved on?

No more grandpa,
No more grandma.
No more aunts,
Not even Mum.
Has time really moved on?

O the pain we bear,

The pain deep inside that's there.

The pain of yesterday,

The pain we are feeling today.

Has time really moved on?

Home of homes is no longer there,

The love and laughter that we'd share,

The affection and attention showing they care.

Prayers of encouragement we would hear.

Has time really moved on?

So many memories created, now captured,

Even the little nuisances we factored.

The bonds we shared now all fractured.

Soon it will mean nothing when raptured.

Has time really moved on?

Maximise the minutes that you have,

Precious moments you cherish and save.

Even at times, have a laugh and a rave.

Challenging times seeking to enslave,

Instruct your demise, so quickly time flies.

Has time really moved on?

54 - Every Day

Walking, running, riding, moving forward every day.

Day by day, no matter what, you are on your way.

The challenges and rigours of life you'd say.

Stop if you must and rest, you're on your way.

Walking, running, riding, moving forward every day.

What a lovely game we play.

A beautiful smile we'd wear each and every day,

Hiding the throb and the aching pain and wishing it away.

Walking, running, riding, moving forward every day.

A crossroad, a diverging place, do I stay?

Scared and confused you'll say?

Which road do I take, which is the right way?

Inform yourself, the outcome it will sway.

Walking, running, riding, moving forward every day.

Indecision just now, you're on your way.

Time moves on, fast or slow it doesn't delay.

Where do I go? Lord help me I pray.

Walking, running, riding, moving forward every day.

Did you just say Lord help me I pray?

Call on Him in the good times and amidst the fray.

Looking ahead, a narrow and winding road is the way.

Walking, running, riding, moving forward every day.

So, challenging it is while on your way.

Invite Him in, a permanent companion to stay,

By your side day by day if you will obey.

Walking, running, riding, moving forward every day.

On Your way, Lord I pray.

Now I know Lord, You are the way.

Give me wisdom and strength for every day.

About the Author

Linley is the third of five children with all his siblings being girls. He was born in London, England. At an early age the family returned to Jamaica and resided in Westmoreland. Linley was an energetic boy who enjoyed the rustic outdoor living.

The family's roots were deeply entrenched in Grange Hill, a sugarcane town where their maternal grandparents resided. Linley and his siblings enjoyed rural life among ordinary country folk all trying to make a living.

Linley attended Munro College, a premier boys' school in the cool hills of St Elizabeth, Jamaica where he boarded. What an experience that was indeed a "city on a hill cannot be hid". It was transformational along with forming lifelong friendships.

Linley worked with the Bank of Nova Scotia Jamaica Limited for more than 37 years and rose to the level of Assistant General Manager. He studied Banking and is qualified to the level of

MBA - Banking and Finance. And is currently a Consultant in Banking and Finance. He has been happily married to Diana for more than 30 years with three adult children: Eleanor, Esther and Emily.

He has committed himself to service within his community and at a national level. He's also an Elder within his local church and throughout his adult life has enjoyed interacting and helping people from all walks of life. He loves to teach others by storytelling always with a focus on their wellbeing.

GLOSSARY

Chamber Pot – also known as chimmey (short for chamber pot), kept under the bed and used for nightly convenience.

Bull kin - a young bull, usually in its intermediary stage of maturity is ideal for butchering, providing soft succulent beef.

Standstill - balancing the bicycle while mounted thereon and bringing it to a total halt. The longer the rider is in this position, the greater the probability of winning the competition.

Edges - the rider performing the risky act of riding very close to a person or an object without touching.

Gig - made from wood in a conical shape and having a metal point in the apex, usually from a nail.

Home Sweet Home - A portable lamp used domestically to provide light prior to having access to electricity. Among the more widely used kerosene oil (paraffin) lamps and lampshades made from glass

Run a Boat - another term for cooking, in this instance illegal cooking on the dormitory

Scorn di eart – playing the gig and catching it, before it touches the ground. The gig spins in the palm of your hand.

Tilley - a type of kerosene lamp for domestic and other use. It uses a gauze to provide very bright light. The kerosene is pressurised by manually pumping it.

Vie - the shortened name for Violet, my mother's first name. Her full name Violet Reynolds

Made in the USA
Columbia, SC
17 June 2024

36794286R00104